Diesel
Detailing Projects

Prototype modeling in HO scale

Selected by Kent Johnson

D1088695

KALMBACH BOOKS

Introduction

The details of a diesel locomotive are much like the proverbial "tip of the iceberg"— providing only a subtle visual hint of the horsepower and engineering concealed inside a hood or carbody and between the truck sideframes. There is, however, a specific reason for the presence and location of each detail item.

The 22 projects in this book provide you with the information you need to accurately model a specific prototype locomotive in HO scale. Modelers in all scales and of varying ability will discover how to enhance the appearance of their diesels by modifying the shell or chassis, adding detail parts, applying accurate paint schemes and decals, weathering, and even installing lighting!

In the following collection of projects from *Model Railroader* Magazine's popular "Paint Shop" column, you'll find a wide variety of prototype roadnames and diesel types to model. Once you select a project, knowledgeable modelers like David Bontrager, Montford Switzer, James Volhard, Andy Sperandeo, Jim Hediger, and Jeff Wilson will provide you with in-depth background information first about the prototype and then the techniques used to model it. Each project also includes a complete list of the parts and materials used.

So whether you're looking to model a specific prototype or just want to explore a variety of useful modeling techniques, read through the articles and quickly see why "the joy is in the details!"

Publisher's Cataloging in Publication
(Prepared by Quality Books Inc.)

Diesel detailing projects : from Model railroader magazine / selected by Kent Johnson.

p. cm.
Includes bibliographical references and index.
ISBN 0-89024-263-1

1. Railroads—Models. 2. Diesel locomotives—Models.
I. Johnson, Kent, 1968– , ed. II. Title: Model railroader.

TF197.D54 1995

625.1'9
QBI95-20106

Contents

Model a Santa Fe Dash 8-40CW in HO scale

The Super Fleet brought back the classic silver and red warbonnet

BY MIKE DANNEMAN

Several years ago I joked with a couple of friends saying how neat it would be if the Atchison, Topeka & Santa Fe would repaint a pair of its cowl-bodied F45s in the classic silver and red warbonnet paint scheme for its business train. I thought it would be a great way for the Santa Fe to nod to its past, which is rich with the history of passenger service headed by the famous *Super Chief*.

The fireman's side features a different handrail arrangement and different details, including the bell in front of the fuel tank.

Fast-forward to today and the joke has become reality. I think many were surprised when the Santa Fe decided to dress a whole fleet of units in this famous color scheme! The railroad now has more than 300 of these warbonnet warriors, including Electro-Motive F45s, GP60Ms, and GP60Bs, and General Electric Dash 8-40BWs and Dash 8-40CWs, pulling everything from their hottest intermodals to coal trains.

As soon as I saw one of Santa Fe's big 800-series Dash 8-40CWs I knew I wanted a model of one. As of August 1993 the railroad had acquired 152 of them, numbered 800-951. When the Rail Power Products Dash 8-40CW shell came out, I quickly grabbed one and took a look at what needed to be done to whip one up in the warbonnet scheme.

At first glance most of the body shell looks really nice, but after looking at the cab I soon realized there was a lot of work ahead of me.

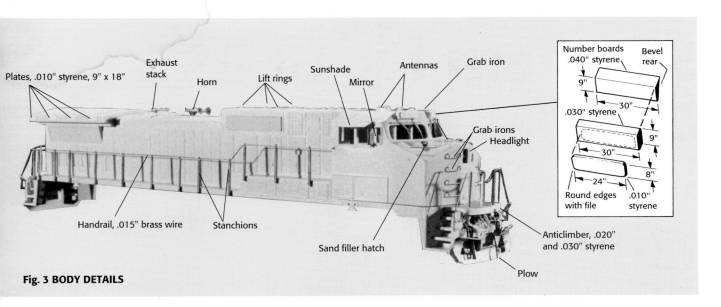

Plates, .010" styrene, 9" x 18"
Exhaust stack
Horn
Lift rings
Sunshade
Mirror
Antennas
Grab iron
Grab irons
Headlight
Number boards
.040" styrene
Bevel rear
9"
30"
.030" styrene
9"
30"
8"
24"
Round edges with file
.010" styrene
Anticlimber, .020" and .030" styrene
Plow
Handrail, .015" brass wire
Stanchions
Sand filler hatch

Fig. 3 BODY DETAILS

would spray the model with light coats from 6" or 7" above the surface. Because of the very quick drying time of Accu-Flex, you must work faster and closer, about 3" from the model, and apply the paint in heavier coats. The sandpaper texture on my first try was caused by some of the paint drying before it hit the surface of the model.

I had two choices: put the model down for a while and cool off, or send the thing to the local landfill after seeing how many pieces an HO scale locomotive could be broken into. Fortunately, cooler heads prevailed. I got the paint off of my model by giving it a bath in Polly S ELO paint stripper. The paint came off cleanly, much to my relief.

It was now time to repaint the model and get it right. I gave the body and cab a coat of Accu-Flex Santa Fe Red, learning my lesson and spraying it closer to the model. The paint looks heavy at first, but as it dries it levels itself nicely

and doesn't hide details. This time I got a beautiful finish, as the paint dried smooth and glossy.

I used masking tape to cover areas that were to remain red, including most of the cab, the warbonnet areas of the hood, and the walkways. The cab roof is red but the hood roof is silver, which is why it's easier to keep them separated until after painting. Because of the paint's quick drying time, the masking can be done very soon. I started masking about a half hour after I sprayed the red. For the warbonnet, I simply photocopied the decal sheet, placed tape gently over it, then cut out the shape of the curve. I sprayed the silver using the same techniques as with the red, with good results. Don't forget to paint the handrails, truck sideframes, and underframe silver.

I brush-painted the wheel faces and couplers with Polly S Roof Brown and the antennas with silver. I also used a

brush to paint the edges of all the window openings with Engine Black. The rear handrails are silver, with yellow at the corners by the steps.

Decals and final details

The Microscale decals went on very well. I had to carefully cut the nose herald to fit around the grab irons on the right side of the nose. I used Micro Sol on each decal, which helped them blend into the surface.

I didn't think the yellow decal areas were bright enough, so I put on a double layer of decals for the yellow striping and nose design. This gave the yellow a much richer look. The front and corner handrails, grab irons, and step edges were then brush-painted with Accu-Flex Santa Fe Yellow.

After everything was dry I installed the handrails and truck sideframes. I gave the whole model a light coat of Blair spray varnish. Artists use this to coat acrylic and oil paintings The varnish has a very nice satin finish, is non-yellowing, and can be found in art supply stores. The Santa Fe keeps its Super Fleet locomotives very clean, so a satin or gloss finish is more appropriate than a dull finish.

The final details, such as headlight lenses, clear styrene windows, and a little exhaust dry-brushed around the stack, finished the model. I now have a nice-looking Santa Fe Dash 8-40CW. Now if I only had room for a layout....

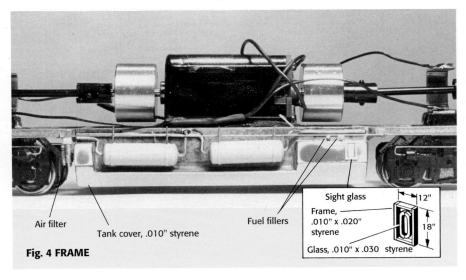

Air filter
Tank cover, .010" styrene
Fuel fillers
Sight glass
12"
Frame, .010" x .020" styrene
18"
Glass, .010" x .030 styrene

Fig. 4 FRAME

Southern Ry. GP49

Tips for painting brass hood units

BY MONTFORD SWITZER
PHOTOS BY THE AUTHOR

The Southern Ry. freight diesel paint scheme is one of my favorites. It's basically black, just as locomotives ought to be. The light gray stripe, often mistaken for white, enhances visibility and the gold lettering and separation stripe classes up the paint job.

I applied Southern's black scheme to an Overland Models Southern Ry. GP49, but even if you aren't painting a Southern Ry. engine, my disassembly and painting techniques might help you with your brass diesel painting project.

Disassembly

Begin by disassembling the model into subassemblies. See fig. 1. The only tools you'll need are a small screwdriver and a screw sticker. I use the screw sticker to put the screws back in their respective holes for painting and safekeeping until reassembly.

Overland locomotives come lubricated and the oils can find their way onto surfaces being painted, ruining the paint's adhesion. To prevent this problem wash everything except the chassis in warm, soapy water to remove any lubricants. Allow ample time for air drying or speed the process with a hair dryer.

Painting

Airbrush Floquil Gray Primer onto the cab interior section of the frame and inside the cab. Brush paint the seat cushions and engineer's control levers Floquil Engine Black. Bake the frame and cab in a kitchen oven for one hour at its lowest setting to cure the paint.

While that's baking, brush Floquil Engine Black on the wheel sides. Since baking would melt the plastic axle insulation, let the paint air dry.

Before painting the exterior surfaces black, mask the cab floor and interior details on the frame so they'll remain gray. Also mask the cab window openings to protect the interior from overspray. Although it may not be absolutely necessary, I also mask the motor and drive train.

Now, airbrush everything with Scalecoat Loco Black. Clean your airbrush to give the paint some setting time, and then remove the masking tape. Let the chassis air dry but bake all other parts.

Gray and gold striping

Whether you paint the gray and gold stripes or use decals for them, the job is much easier on models with hoods and a cab that are removable from the frame. I

Lowell Suttman

Here's a shot of a prototype GP49 in the Southern Ry. scheme. Most of these units are now painted for the Southern's successor, Norfolk Southern.

used the one-piece Microscale gray and gold decal stripes. The bottom of the gray stripe should be 10½" above the top of the lowest walkway or even with the raised walkway.

I added stripes to the long and short hoods first, starting with the ends, but avoiding the areas under the grab irons. Then I cut pieces of decal stripe to fit under the grab irons and slid them into place. This turned out to be a tricky operation and I'm lucky it came out okay.

In retrospect it would've been easier to unsolder the grab irons, apply the decal stripe in a continuous run, and

Fig. 1 MODEL DISASSEMBLY. With everything apart the model should look like this. Reinsert the screws into the holes they came from for safekeeping. This also ensures they'll be painted the appropriate color.

Bill of materials

Evergreen
9005	.005" clear styrene

Floquil
110009	Gray Primer
110010	Engine Black
110013	Grimy Black
110074	Boxcar Red

Kadee
5	couplers

Microscale
87124-6	HO 1" and 2" yellow stripes
87539	Southern hood unit decals
87540	Southern hood unit stripes

MV Products
22	headlight lenses

Polly S
410031	Reefer Yellow
120073	Rust

Scalecoat
10	Loco Black
23	Silver

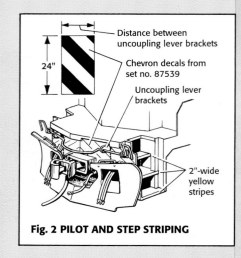

Fig. 2 PILOT AND STEP STRIPING

- Distance between uncoupling lever brackets
- Chevron decals from set no. 87539
- Uncoupling lever brackets
- 2"-wide yellow stripes
- 24"

then reattach the grabs using cyanoacrylate adhesive (CA).

Temporarily set the hoods and cab on the frame so you'll be able to match the stripes on the cab and battery boxes to those on the hoods. Apply the decals, let them dry, and then slit the stripe to allow removal of the cab. Slit the gold striping off the top of the battery box stripe and use it around the front and rear of the cab. Also apply pieces of gray striping around the front and rear of the battery boxes. Cutting small slits in the decals for the step grab irons will work well here.

Chevrons and number boards

Decal chevrons on the pilots always present a challenge but they're really difficult on this model because of the permanently affixed details including snow plows. The solution is to cut the chevrons into three sections and apply them individually around the permanent details. See fig. 2 They need to be only 24" tall since the snow plows cover the lower pilots.

Make the number board backing from scrap .010" styrene – it's easier to install than the brass pieces provided with the model. Glue them in place with CA and paint them black with a brush. When dry, apply the decal numbers from the Microscale set.

Add the equipment trust plate and builders plate decals as shown in the finished model photo. Check all the decals for bubbles, pierce any you find with a model knife, and apply another dose of decal setting solution.

Hand-painted details

The best time to do the hand painting is before reassembly of the components. Apply Scalecoat Silver paint to the cab-side window frames, windshield wipers, air and m.u. hose glad hands, headlight covers, and step lights.

Paint the brake shoes with Polly S Rust. Use Polly S Reefer Yellow on the handrails. Water-based Polly S gives one-coat coverage and you can wipe away mistakes using a soft damp cloth. Use Microscale 2"-wide yellow decal stripes cut to the various lengths for the step edges. See fig. 2.

Insert the loose wind deflectors that come with the model in the holes on the engineer's side only. Bend the tabs to hold them in place and add a spot of CA as insurance.

Finishing up

Airbrush all components except the chassis, fuel tank, and truck side frames with Floquil Clear Gloss for a semigloss finish. This looks about right for a well-maintained Southern diesel. When the Clear Gloss is dry, mask the three air intake openings on each side of the long hood and spray them with Floquil Grimy Black for a dirty appearance.

Weather the fuel tank and truck side frames with an overspray of Floquil Grimy Black. This can be a heavy application since these areas get dirty fast even on the cleanest locomotives.

This is a good time to dirty the carbody roof as well. Give it a thin overspray of Floquil boxcar red to add a convincing rust and dirt tone. Create the

fuel spills at the fuel fill locations by running a small paint brush loaded with lacquer thinner through the layers of weathering. The glossy base coat will reappear mixed with the grimy black and boxcar red to make a convincing fuel spill.

Set all the components aside for a couple of days to let all the paint and weathering dry completely. Take advantage of this time to install the .005" clear plastic window material and MV Products headlight lenses using white glue. The white glue dries clear so if any gets on a visible surface, just leave it there.

To model the lenses, fill the class light openings with white glue. Add Kadee no. 5 couplers painted with Floquil Rust.

Although the model is still in ten pieces the hard work is done. Tape the ends of the handrails so they won't scratch the cab and carefully reassemble the components. Then adjust the Kadee coupler "air hoses" and test run the unit.

You now have a model of one of the last locomotives to get the classic Southern Ry. paint scheme, just before the 1982 Norfolk Southern merger. This is one black-and-white paint scheme that I'm glad to see will live on in our hearts and basements.

Build a Conrail General Electric B23-7

Subtle weathering enhances the appearance of this relatively spartan Conrail B23-7 road switcher by bringing out such details as the brake chain, sand pipes, and truck springs.

An accurate modern diesel without major surgery

BY DAVID BONTRAGER
PHOTOS BY THE AUTHOR

GENERAL ELECTRIC'S B23-7 is a 2,250-hp B-B road switcher introduced as part of GE's Dash 7 locomotive line in 1977. It's an intermediate-size, general-purpose locomotive, so the B23-7 competed directly with Electro-Motive Division's GP38-2. The B23-7s are used for anything from local switching to high-speed mainline trips.

The B23-7 has the distinctive extended radiator housing and stepped out rear hood characteristic of GE's Dash 7 line. Other smaller details vary from order to order, so I studied numerous reference photos to choose the parts for my Conrail B23-7.

CONRAIL UNITS

According to the first edition of *Diesel Locomotive Rosters: U. S., Canada, Mexico* (Kalmbach Publishing Co.), Conrail originally owned 141 B23-7s numbered 1900-2023 and 2800-2816. These units were built between 1977 and 1979. The third edition of *Diesel Locomotive Rosters* shows 134 units remaining in 1992, numbered 1900-1902, 1910-2023, and 2800-2816.

These units ride on AAR type B trucks and have normal Dash 7 hood louvers. The battery box doors, extra cab side windows, type of horn, antenna, exhaust, and electrical box are common items on Conrail's units. There's some variation in the snowplow pilots, and some units have the horns in different positions. Judging from photos, the right-side horn location is the most common.

Most of my previous modeling articles involve western prototypes, so you may be wondering what I'm doing with

Thanks to a run-through agreement, Conrail's blue and white scheme makes an appearance in the rugged Rocky Mountains on the author's HO layout.

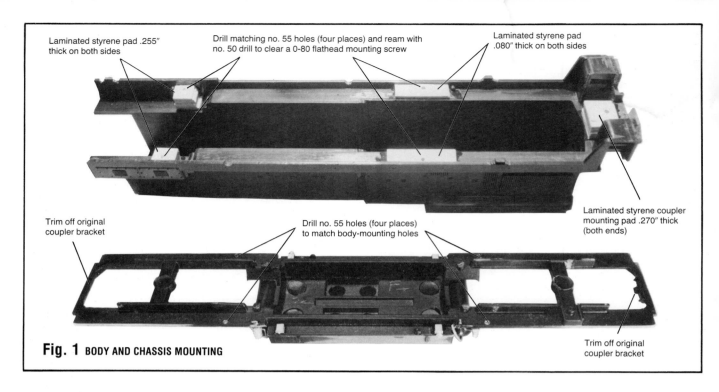

Laminated styrene pad .255" thick on both sides

Drill matching no. 55 holes (four places) and ream with no. 50 drill to clear a 0-80 flathead mounting screw

Laminated styrene pad .080" thick on both sides

Laminated styrene coupler mounting pad .270" thick (both ends)

Trim off original coupler bracket

Drill no. 55 holes (four places) to match body-mounting holes

Trim off original coupler bracket

Fig. 1 BODY AND CHASSIS MOUNTING

a Conrail unit. The answer is nostalgia. I grew up in northern Indiana and watched the New York Central, then Penn Central, and finally Conrail. I always admired Conrail's paint scheme and planned to build a "Big Blue" diesel, but the project kept getting put off

in favor of something else. The new B23-7 body from Rail Power Products put the project back into high gear.

A BETTER HO SHELL

The RPP B23-7 shell is made from upgraded tooling with better detail

than the firm's earlier efforts. It has the correct proportions and will fit any Athearn four-axle GE chassis. A standard GE cab, with single windows on each side, comes with the body. The RPP cab is interchangeable with Athearn's GE cab that includes the optional extra

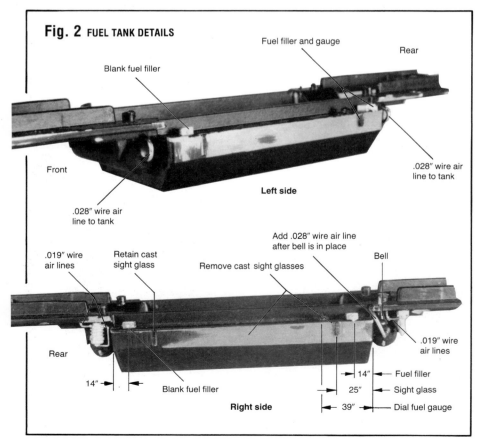

Fig. 2 FUEL TANK DETAILS

Fuel filler and gauge

Rear

Blank fuel filler

Front

Left side

.028" wire air line to tank

.028" wire air line to tank

.019" wire air lines

Retain cast sight glass

Add .028" wire air line after bell is in place

Bell

Remove cast sight glasses

.019" wire air lines

Rear

14"

Blank fuel filler

14" — Fuel filler

25" — Sight glass

39" — Dial fuel gauge

Right side

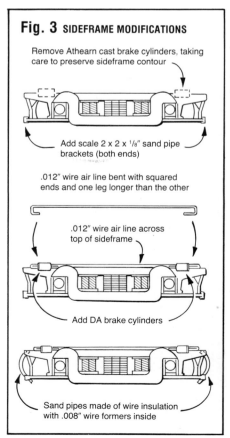

Fig. 3 SIDEFRAME MODIFICATIONS

Remove Athearn cast brake cylinders, taking care to preserve sideframe contour

Add scale 2 x 2 x 1/8" sand pipe brackets (both ends)

.012" wire air line bent with squared ends and one leg longer than the other

.012" wire air line across top of sideframe

Add DA brake cylinders

Sand pipes made of wire insulation with .008" wire formers inside

side windows. By switching cabs, you end up with an easy choice of side window arrangements.

I built my B23-7 as a dummy unit, but the same detailing techniques can be used for a powered locomotive. For a powered model, I'd recommend the Athearn or Proto Power West mechanisms.

PROTOTYPE AND MODEL DETAILS

Conrail's locomotives tend to be rather spartan, with few extra-cost options. Its B23-7s do have the extra cab side windows, so I used an Athearn cab. The balance of the details follows standard Conrail or GE practices, so building this model is a straightforward detailing project with only a few modifications to the chassis or body.

At one time I liked to use bits of brass wire to reinforce small parts. Since then, I've learned that plastic rod works better. Drill a no. 76 hole in the back of the part and cement it to a piece of .020" styrene rod with liquid plastic cement. Drill another no. 76 hole through the body, press the part into place, and apply liquid plastic cement from inside the shell. Capillary action carries the cement through the hole to secure the part while the rod keeps it from shifting. After the cement has set hard, trim off the excess rod with flush-cutting pliers.

BODY MOUNTING

Begin the project by modifying the B23-7 body so it can be attached to the frame. I use machine screws that pass through the running boards and thread into the frame. Flathead screws, countersunk into the running boards, aren't noticeable, and the metal frame holds threads better than plastic does. When the time comes for maintenance or repairs, I can remove the detailed body with minimal handling. I just set the model on the workbench, remove the screws, and lift off the body.

Figure 1 shows the details of my body-mounting system. Install laminated styrene pads beneath the running boards in four locations. The thicknesses specified for these pads set the model's overall height. With the frame in the body, mark the four pilot hole locations. Drill these frame holes first, keeping them as far outboard as possible. Slip the frame into the body, check its position, and drill the matching holes up through the mounting pads and running boards. Be careful to keep these holes vertical.

Separate the parts and scribe an "F" and an "R" into the frame to indicate front and rear. Ream the holes through the running boards and body-mounting pads with a no. 50 drill so the 0-80 mounting screws will have a slip fit. Use a larger drill bit to countersink these holes until the flathead screws are flush with the running boards.

This is also a good time to add the styrene mounting pads for the couplers. Laminate pads of styrene and cement them behind each pilot as shown in fig. 1. Use the top of a Kadee no. 5 draft-gear box as a pattern to locate holes for the draft-gear mounting screws. Drill mounting holes into the styrene blocks, but don't mount the couplers until final assembly.

CHASSIS DETAILS

Prototype locomotives have a fascinating array of piping and equipment around the fuel tank. A few detail parts and some bits of wire here will add a lot of realism for relatively little effort.

Cement the Athearn air tanks together, let them dry, and sand the joint lines smooth. You may have to use body filler to cover any gaps. Drill the ends of the tanks with a no. 70 bit and add air lines as shown in fig. 2.

Smooth the right side of the fuel tank with a file, leaving the rear fuel sight glass but removing the other two. Add a blank fuel filler by cutting the neck off the Details West part, filing it smooth, and adding a nut-bolt-washer casting. Add the bell and install the front air line around it.

My Conrail B23-7 is a dummy, but I still like to use NorthWest Short Line or Jay-Bee nickel-silver wheelsets for improved appearance. If you change wheels, be sure to check the clearance between the new parts and the originals. I had to trim the axle end off the

outer face of the wheels with a cutoff disk in a motor tool.

TRUCK SIDEFRAMES

Athearn's truck sideframes look great, but their molded air cylinders are a bit bulky. Shave off these details, being careful to avoid damaging the sideframe. Replace them with Detail Associates air cylinders as shown in fig. 3.

Drill a no. 80 hole into the end of each brake cylinder for the air pipe. Form this pipe from .012" brass wire so it has squared corners and one end longer than the other. See fig. 3. Slip the long end into one brake cylinder, pushing it all the way in to allow room for the other end to slip over the opposite air cylinder and enter the pipe hole. Center the air line and lay it on top of the sideframe parallel with the back. Then secure the pipe with a drop of cyanoacrylate adhesive (CA).

Bits of 1/2"-long electrical insulation simulate the sand pipes at each end of the sideframes. See fig. 3. Slip pieces of .008" brass wire into the insulation so the pipe will hold its shape. Pull the .008" wire out of the top end of the insulation and bend it 90 degrees. Drill a no. 80 hole into the back of the sideframe,

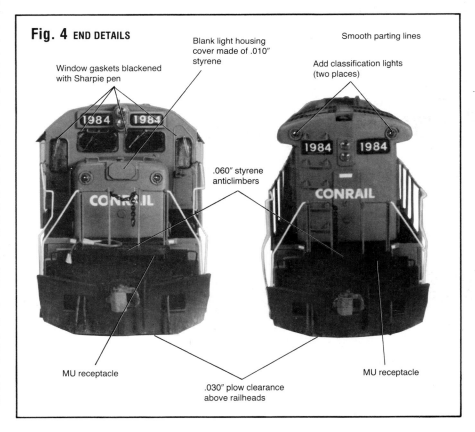

Fig. 4 END DETAILS

Window gaskets blackened with Sharpie pen

Blank light housing cover made of .010" styrene

Smooth parting lines

Add classification lights (two places)

.060" styrene anticlimbers

MU receptacle

MU receptacle

.030" plow clearance above railheads

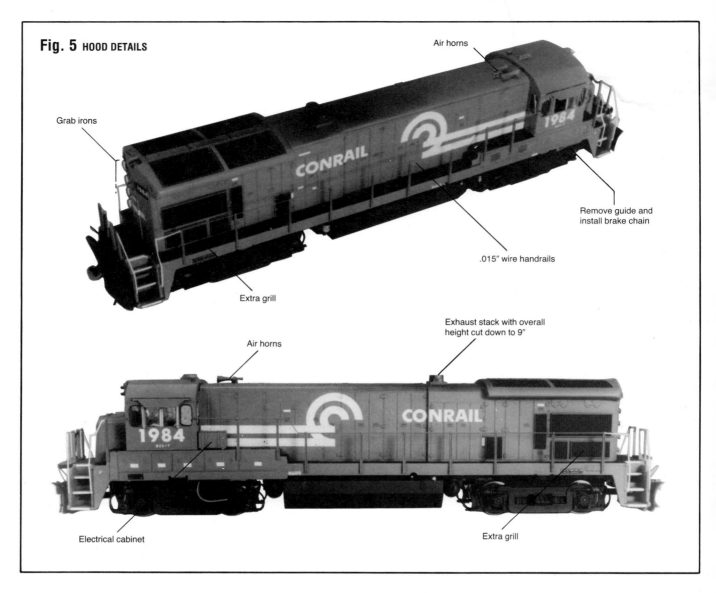

Fig. 5 HOOD DETAILS

Air horns

Grab irons

Remove guide and install brake chain

.015" wire handrails

Extra grill

Exhaust stack with overall height cut down to 9"

Air horns

Electrical cabinet

Extra grill

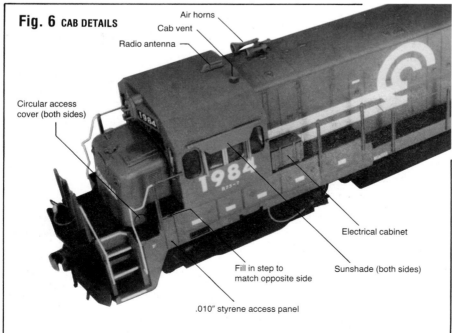

Fig. 6 CAB DETAILS

Air horns

Cab vent

Radio antenna

Circular access cover (both sides)

Electrical cabinet

Fill in step to match opposite side

Sunshade (both sides)

.010" styrene access panel

near the top corner, and press the bent leg into the hole. A drop of CA will secure the pipe at both ends. Then trim off the bottom of the pipe parallel with the rails (about a 30-degree angle).

END DETAILS

Conrail locomotives use a variety of snowplows, even among units within the same model class and number series. With this in mind, I selected a typical plow and used it on both ends. See fig. 4. You may prefer to substitute one of the other types.

Next, drill the holes for the pilot details and test-fit the pieces without cement. Install the uncoupling levers with wire eyebolts. Then mount the parts "dry" and use CA to attach the lever to the eyebolts. Once the CA has set, remove the uncoupling lever as a subassembly for painting.

Use .015" brass wire for the handrails and bend them to fit your unit. I used the diagrams in the RPP instructions and Conrail photos as guides.

HOOD DETAILS

The RPP B23-7 includes the basic GE radiator grills in the body casting and supplies the optional grills as separate pieces. General Electric has used several grill combinations on the different B23-7 orders, so it's a good idea to check prototype pictures to make sure you use the right ones. Scrape off any details that interfere, and cement the extra grills to the body with liquid plastic cement, as shown in fig. 5. Save the unused grills for future projects.

An Athearn EMD air horn assembly is close to the type used by Conrail. Remove the mold parting lines and file the front of each trumpet smooth and flat. Be careful with the small rear trumpet as it bends easily. Drill a no. 76 hole dead center into the two large trumpets and a no. 78 hole in the small trumpet. Make these holes deep, but don't drill through the rear of the casting. Open up the bell of each trumpet using nos. 50, 52, and 57 bits respectively on the large, medium, and small bells. Try to get the opening as large as possible without distorting the bell shape.

Once you've finished the horns, remove the cast brace between the front trumpets. Taper the frame and attach the assembly to a piece of .040" plastic rod with liquid cement. This rod becomes the mounting pin after everything has set hard.

CAB DETAILS

Choosing a headlight casting is a problem. The Precision Scale one I used (see fig. 6) doesn't have GE's correct rectangular shape, though it does have the light shields that I consider more important. Detail Associates no. 1003 is a nice rectangular headlight, but it lacks the shields and adding them is tedious.

Window glazing may be done in several ways. Most observers don't notice if the cab windows are set flush with the exterior wall, so clear glazing cemented inside the openings works fine. Flush-mounted windows are more realistic if a model will be scrutinized. Use thick clear styrene and the cut-and-fit method to make individual panes for each window opening. As you finish each piece, stick it to a masking-tape label and set the glazing aside for installation after you've painted the model.

To make the cab windows more realistic, use a Sharpie marking pen to darken the gaskets. Then paint the inside of each opening black.

A-Line's windshield wipers are probably the best HO wipers ever produced, but they're extremely fragile. Be careful as you cut them from the sprue and during handling. These wipers are cast in a flexible engineering plastic, so install them by gently pressing them into no. 78 holes.

Bill of materials

Athearn
3440 U30B powered locomotive kit, undecorated
3450 U30B dummy locomotive kit, undecorated

A-Line (Proto Power West)
292000 windshield wipers

Builders In Scale
250 black chain, 40 links per inch

Detail Associates
1019 class light knockouts
1202 bell
1301 sunshades
1403 GE drop step
1507 m.u. receptacles
1508 m.u. hoses
1708 class light lenses
1709 headlight lenses
1803 antenna
1901 roof vent
2206 eyebolts
2212 uncoupling levers
2304 wind deflectors
2306 electrical cabinet
2307 circular access cover
2502 .008" brass wire
2504 .012" brass wire
2505 .015" brass wire
2506 .019" brass wire
2508 .028" brass wire
2801 air cylinders
2808 GE speed recorder
3001 sand filler hatch

Details West
139 air filter set
149 fuel fillers

Evergreen Scale Models styrene
159 .060" x .250" strip
8202 2 x 2 strip
9010 .010" sheet
9015 .015" sheet
9020 .020" sheet
9030 .030" sheet
9040 .040" sheet
9060 .060" sheet

Jay-Bee
102 40" replacement wheels for powered locomotives
109 40" replacement wheels for dummy trucks

Kadee
5 couplers

Microscale
60-70-1 small letters and numbers
87-48 diesel data
87-157 Conrail locomotive decal set

Model Power
384-A small bulb, insulation used for sand pipes

NorthWest Short Line
71314 40" nickel-silver wheelsets for dummy locomotive
71414 40" nickel-silver stub-axle wheels for powered locomotives

Precision Scale
3150 air supply hoses
3934 headlight
3997 door latches
39011 fuel sight glass
39037 dial fuel gauge
39055 plow pilot-front and rear
39059 m.u. hose kit (use brackets only)

Rail Power Products
GE B23-7 body shell kit

Scalecoat II paint
2010 black
2075 Conrail blue

Smokey Valley Railroad & Machine
110 GE handrail stanchions

Testor
1260 Dullcote

Tichy Train Group
3015 drop style grab irons
3021 straight style grab irons

Miscellaneous
body putty
cyanoacrylate adhesive
decal-setting solution
liquid plastic cement

CONRAIL

PAINTING

Painting this model is easy using Scalecoat II, a plastic-compatible paint that dries to a glossy surface ideal for decaling. The body and cab are Conrail Blue with black pilots, running boards, fuel tank, and truck sideframes.

After the paint has dried, apply the lettering using decal setting solution to soften the film so it will conform to the details. Use bits of extra Conrail logos to trim the step edges. I made the small "B23-7" on the cab side by using scale 3" letters that came from Microscale's N scale decal set no. 60-70-1. Builder's plates and other data are in that firm's diesel data set.

FINAL STEPS

When the lettering has dried, apply a light coat of Testor's Dullcote thinned 1:1 with lacquer thinner for the airbrush. Do the final assembly, and add light weathering with drybrushing and powdered chalks.

A final light application of Dullcote comes next. All that's left is to install the windows and lenses. Now your unit's ready to roll. ✿

Maroon and gold F3

Paint an HO scale cab unit in the Soo Line's early scheme

BY JEFF WILSON

Chris Becker

The Soo Line's early maroon and gold scheme ranks as one of my all-time favorites. This scheme was used from the late 1940s until 1961, when the Minneapolis, St. Paul & Sault Ste. Marie, the Wisconsin Central, and the Duluth, South Shore & Atlantic merged to officially create the Soo Line. Red and white became the road's new colors, but locomotives could still be found in the old scheme through the late '60s.

During the late 1940s and 1950s, the MStP&SSM and affiliate WC acquired a fleet of 57 Electro-Motive Division F units. A two-part article on Soo F units appeared in vol. 1, nos. 1 and 2 of *The Soo*, the newsletter of the Soo Line Historical Society. It includes painting diagrams, rosters, and information on detail variations.

The Soo was notorious for playing Erector Set with its F units. Locomotives often had side louver panels, air grills, and other details modified. Both prototype photos show this, as no. 2203-A has had one of its horizontal sets of louvers replaced with vertical ones, and no. 203-A

has lost one set of louvers completely. I chose to model 203-A, a Phase IV F3, as it appeared in the early 1960s.

Shell modifications

Since the Phase IV F3 (sometimes termed an F5) has many of the same details as an early F7, I started with an undecorated Athearn F7. Begin by removing the shell from the frame. I used a small cutting bit (Dremel no. 194) in my motor tool to remove the steam generator details on the rear roof hatch, the dynamic brake fan (on the hatch immediately behind the cab), and the exhaust stacks. By working slowly and removing a small amount of material with each pass, I managed to leave a fairly smooth surface. (You can use a hobby knife if you don't have a motor tool.) I completed the job by wet-sanding the hatch areas with 600-grit sandpaper. The spark arrestors hide any marks around the stacks.

I contemplated replacing the Athearn number boxes, but a little carving with a hobby knife as shown in fig. 1 improved their appearance.

Then I used a chisel-point blade to

Soo Line (former Wisconsin Central) F7 2203-A still wears the maroon and gold paint scheme in March 1967. Wisconsin Central units carried tiny "WC" initials, which can be seen just below the air grill at the rear of the engine.

Jim Shepard collection

Soo Line F-unit roster

Number	Model
200-A, B	F3A Phase II
201-202-A, B	F3A Phase III
203-204-A, B	F3A Phase IV
212-A, B	F7A Phase I
213-214-A, B	F7A Phase II
500-503-A	FP7A Phase I
500-503-C	F7B Phase I
504-505	FP7A Phase II
2200-A, B	F3A Phase IV
2200-C	F3B Phase IV
2201-2203-A, B	F7A Phase I
2201-2203-C	F7B Phase I
2204-C	F7B Phase II
2224-2227-A, B	F7A Phase I
2228-2230-A, B	F7A Phase II
2500-2501-A	FP7A Phase I
2500-2501-C	F7B Phase I

Minneapolis, St. Paul & Sault Ste. Marie locomotives have three-digit numbers; Wisconsin Central units have four-digit numbers.

Jim Scribbins

Soo Line F3 no. 203-A pulls a train north of Slinger, Wis., in June 1963, two years before the locomotive was traded in to EMD.

remove the forward louvers from the fireman's side of the shell. I failed to notice (until the paint was dry, of course) that I should have removed the water hatches from both sides as shown in fig. 2.

I cut windshields to fit using .015" clear styrene. I made templates for each piece using thin cardstock, then traced these onto the clear styrene. Then I set the windshields aside.

Next, I used a hobby knife and sandpaper to clean up mold-parting lines on the roof, pilot, side of the nose, and below the headlight. I scribed a line just above the anticlimber to complete the outline of the nose door.

I drilled holes for the antenna, lift rings, windshield wipers, spark arrestors, and grab irons. To locate the nose grab irons, I placed masking tape on the nose and marked the locations with a pencil. I used cyanoacrylate adhesive (CA) to glue the spark arrestors, antenna, horns, and lift rings in place.

You can use the Athearn draft-gear boxes for Kadee couplers, but I find the couplers work much better in their own draft-gear boxes. I mounted the front coupler on the shell as shown in fig. 3.

Frame

I removed the mounting bracket for the headlight and the strip-metal contact pieces. I replaced these with wire as shown in fig. 4 for better electrical contact.

The front coupler mount was removed with a hacksaw to make room for a shell-mounted coupler. I mounted the rear coupler as shown in fig. 5.

Painting

I washed the shell in warm water with a bit of liquid dishwashing detergent, used a toothbrush to scrub it, then rinsed it under running water. I used an airbrush (without paint) to blow water off the model and prevent water spots from marring the surface. Then I let the shell sit overnight to dry completely.

This model is painted with Badger's water-based Accu-Flex paint. If you have not yet discovered Accu-Flex, I encourage you to give it a try, though you might have to adjust your painting style a bit. The secret to getting a good finish with Accu-Flex is to use about 35 pounds of pressure, get in tight to the model (about 2"), and put the paint on wet. Using a good internal-mix airbrush will also help. (I've used a Badger 200 with excellent results.) The paint doesn't require thinning.

The paint levels nicely and settles beautifully around details. Applying the paint in light coats can result in a pebbled or orange-peel surface. If you feel uncomfortable spraying heavy coats, practice on a boxcar shell or scrap piece first. You shouldn't have to apply more than two coats for complete coverage.

I cut masking tape to fit over the upper

air intake grill on each side, where the etched-steel grills will go. Then I sprayed the entire body with Soo Line Maroon.

The paint dries very quickly. In fact, you can mask and apply a second color 20 minutes after the first. To speed up the drying time and give the paint an extra-hard finish, I went over the model with a hair dryer for a minute. Badger recommends this, and I've had good results doing it. Be careful not to get the model too hot – melting plastic isn't fun.

The pilot, fuel tank skirts, and most of the rear (see fig. 6) are black. I used masking tape and paper to cover the areas that will stay maroon, then sprayed the rest, including the assembled truck sideframes, with Engine Black. Then I removed the tape and used the hair dryer on the black areas. I also used black to brush-paint the tank and the shiny metal inner truck frames. I brush-painted the sides of the wheels Grimy Black.

Side stripes and decals

The Microscale decal set provides the large imitation gold nose piece in two halves that taper to the scale 12" width of the side stripes. I used masking tape, cut with a knife on a piece of glass to ensure a clean edge, to mask around the stripe from the front steps to the rear on each side. The stripes wrap around the end as shown in fig. 6. I also masked off the anticlimber. I used both tape and

17

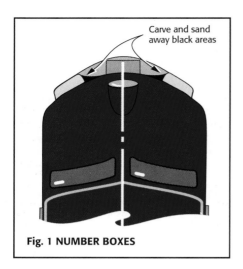

Fig. 1 NUMBER BOXES

Carve and sand away black areas

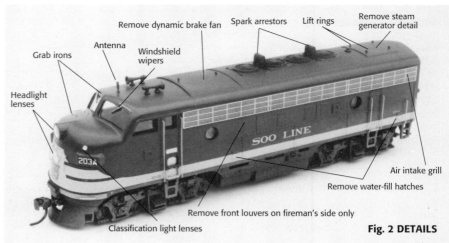

Fig. 2 DETAILS

Grab irons
Antenna
Windshield wipers
Remove dynamic brake fan
Spark arrestors
Lift rings
Remove steam generator detail
Headlight lenses
Remove steam generator detail
Air intake grill
Remove water-fill hatches
Classification light lenses
Remove front louvers on fireman's side only

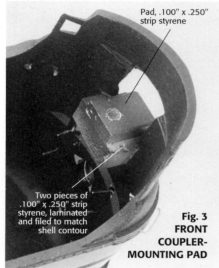

Pad, .100" x .250" strip styrene

Two pieces of .100" x .250" strip styrene, laminated and filed to match shell contour

Fig. 3 FRONT COUPLER-MOUNTING PAD

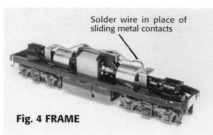

Solder wire in place of sliding metal contacts

Fig. 4 FRAME

Fig. 5. REAR COUPLER. Cut the ears off a Kadee no. 27 coupler box and use five-minute epoxy to secure the box to the frame.

Fig. 6. REAR. The gold stripes and maroon body color wrap around the rear of the body. The remainder of the rear is black.

Bill of materials

Accu-Flex paint
16-1 Engine Black
16-3 Grimy Black
16-18 Soo Line Maroon
16-19 Soo Line Dulux Gold
16-30 Sand
16-32 Santa Fe Silver

Athearn
3223 F7 undecorated

Detail Associates
701 detail set
2202 grab irons
2704 air intake grills

Evergreen styrene
109 .100" x .250" strip
9007 .015" clear sheet

Kadee
8 coupler
27 coupler

Microscale
87-48 diesel data decals
87-116 Soo Line early diesel decals
MI-1 Micro Set
MI-2 Micro Sol
MI-9 Micro Kristal Klear

MV Products
11 headlight lenses
22 classification light lenses

Overland Models
9572 spark arrestors

Precision Scale Co.
3968 Windshield Wipers

ShellScale decal
105 EMD white insert-style numbers

Testor Corp.
1959 Model Master Semi-Gloss Clear Lacquer

paper to cover the rest of the body, then sprayed the stripes and anticlimber with Soo Line Dulux Gold.

I started applying decals with the two-part nose piece. Before soaking the decal, I set one half in place, marked the location of the lower headlight, and cut out this area. Experience showed me that this helps keep the decal from becoming distorted at the top. Then I floated the piece from the decal sheet onto a puddle of Micro Set. The bottom of the decals must be kept even with the bottom edge of the painted side stripes. Once the decal was in place, I used the corner of a paper towel to soak up the excess Micro Set, then applied Micro Sol, which helped the decal conform to the nose contour.

When the first half had dried, I applied the second in the same manner, butting it against the first. Since these pieces don't quite reach the steps, I cut some gold material from another area on the decal sheet to fit between the end of the decal and the step on each side. The paint and decal colors aren't an exact match, so I wanted to keep the joint between the two at the steps. However, the color difference isn't very noticeable, especially after a bit of weathering.

Once the nose decals had dried I used a sharp hobby knife to slice along the outline of the nose door. I also used the knife to poke any bubbles in the decals, then added more Micro Sol. I repeated this process until the decals were snugly in place on the body.

I added the nose herald and the ShellScale number board decals. ShellScale makes beautiful number board decals; unfortunately, they don't include letters. I scavenged the "A" decals from an old Champion set in my scrap box.

The side decals were next, including the thin black stripes, road name, small numbers, and EMD builder's plate (from Microscale set no. 87-48). Take your time with the thin stripes. If a piece just doesn't want to go on straight, peel it off, throw it away, and start over.

I glued the new air grills in place with small dabs of acrylic matte medium. This material dries clear and flat, so it won't be seen beneath the etched panels.

Final details and weathering

I used a fine-point brush and Accu-Flex Santa Fe Silver to paint the kick-plates in the steps on each side. The grab irons were painted with Dulux Gold, then installed. The handle on the nose door is a small piece of .012" wire painted gold.

I weathered the model lightly, spraying a light coat of Engine Black on the spark arrestors and around the fans on the roof. Then I used Sand to dust the trucks and side of the locomotive, starting just behind the pilot. I finished with a light coat of Grimy Black on the trucks, fuel tank, and pilot.

When the paint had dried, I gave the shell a light coat of Testor's Model Master Semi-Gloss Clear lacquer to seal everything. I used a brush to give the couplers a light coat of Polly S 410070 Roof Brown.

The windshields are held in place with drops of Micro Kristal Klear applied from the inside. I painted the windshield wipers silver and black and added them, along with the side window glazing and headlight and classification light lenses. After snapping the shell to the frame and adding the front coupler, my locomotive was set to pull the next Soo Line freight across Wisconsin.

A. L. Schmidt

Chicago & North Western's ex-Conrail GP40s

Paint a unit in the 1980s Pentone Yellow scheme

BY JAMES VOLHARD

The Chicago & North Western bought its fleet of 38 GP40s, nos. 5500-5537, from Conrail in 1980 as used locomotives. Built in 1965 for the New York Central, these units are among the oldest of their kind. The C&NW rebuilt them in its Oelwein, Iowa, shops in 1980-81, intending to use them in the high-horsepower locomotive pool on the Chicago-Omaha main line.

However, the early-1980s recession and their less-than-reliable performance caused many of these units to spend time in storage. By the mid-'80s several of them could be found running on the Wisconsin Division and other secondary main lines. The 1990s found many GP40s in storage, but they've been placed back in service occasionally when traffic picks up.

The obvious choice for modeling this engine in HO scale seemed to be the Con-Cor GP40, but then I took a closer look at Athearn's GP40-2. The differences between the GP40 and the GP40-2 are minor. Some components are shifted a few inches this way or that, but I decided I could live with those discrepancies because of the better overall detail of the Athearn shell and the running compatibility with my mostly Athearn fleet.

Body modifications

I began by completely disassembling the model. Starting with the frame I drilled the required holes on both sides of the fuel tank for the fuel fillers and gauges. I also cut off the coupler-mounting pads, as I mount my couplers on the shell. After smoothing any rough spots on the fuel tank with a mill file and sandpaper, I

attached the fuel fillers and gauges to the tank with cyanoacrylate adhesive (CA).

The prototype has the older GP-type or "Blomberg B" truck sideframes, so I used Athearn early sideframes and removed the outboard brake shoes. I drilled the ends of the brake cylinders with a no. 80 drill. Then I formed brake piping from .012" brass wire and glued it in place with CA as shown in fig. 1. Next, I airbrushed the completed frame and trucks with Scalecoat Black and set them aside to dry.

The coupler-mounting pads are styrene tiles 1/4" square and .040" thick. I broke the tiles apart and stacked them five high from the bottom of the floor, gluing them with liquid plastic cement. Then I assembled the Kadee couplers in their draft-gear boxes, using a no. 26 coupler on the front and a no. 5 coupler on the rear. The side ears and rear of the draft-gear box must be trimmed off to clear both the pilot and frame.

Next, I drilled no. 50 mounting holes and tapped them for 2-56 screws. Then I mounted the couplers, snapped the body to the reassembled frame, and checked the coupler height. It came out perfect for me, but you can adjust the pad height by filing it down or adding more styrene. After removing the shell, I removed the couplers and set them aside for a while.

To backdate the shell, I filled the water sight glass on the engineer's side of the long hood with putty. When it had dried I scraped and wet-sanded the area until it was smooth. The roof fans came next. Removing the fans would have destroyed some of the detail. Besides, the depth of the Athearn fan detail is incredible. Instead, I used a knife to cut scale 24"-diameter disks from .010" styrene and glued them to the fan centers as shown in fig. 1.

I modified the cab by trimming the angled overhang on the rear roofline flush with the rear wall of the cab. I also cut off the cab vent on the fireman's side and wet-sanded the area smooth. Next, I glued on the radio antenna and drilled the hole for the horn.

I removed the access door and battery box cover from below the cab on the left side as shown in fig. 2. These are replaced with the appropriate parts from an Athearn GP35 shell. I used a razor saw to cut the access door off the GP35 body, then filed it to match the thickness of the one I sliced off the GP40-2 shell. The battery box cover is a snap-on part, so I trimmed off the mounting pin and set it aside to be glued on after painting.

I cut a hole in the nose to mount the bell, as shown in fig. 2, by first drilling a 1/8" hole through the nose, then enlarging the hole to the required size with flat and square needle files.

The top corners of the pilots have a 10"-square notch removed. I filled in the rear pilot below the coupler with styrene sheet to match the rest of the pilot. I drilled mounting holes for the lift rings, grab irons, cut levers, and m.u. hoses, then used CA to mount the plow, air filters, lift rings, grab irons, m.u. receptacles, drop steps, and uncoupling levers to the body.

Painting

A little knowledge of the prototype is necessary for painting the GP40. Some units were painted in the yellow and green scheme using the darker yellow color, as seen in the prototype photo. Others were painted with the then-new Pentone 102C Yellow (sometimes called "Safety Yellow" or "Zito Yellow"). The Pentone Yellow was standard from 1982 until July 1991, when the C&NW returned to the traditional darker yellow paint.

The 102C yellow units didn't follow a specific numerical sequence, but were distributed throughout the roster. I recommend working from a photo or other prototype information to paint your unit the proper color.

I modeled no. 5517, one of the Pentone Yellow units (others included 5503, 5510, 5512, 5513, 5517, and 5520). To represent this color I added 25 percent Scalecoat White to the CNW Yellow. This isn't a perfect match for a freshly painted engine, but it's quite accurate for an older unit as this yellow faded (sometimes quite drastically) with age.

I airbrushed Floquil Primer, thinned with 25 percent Dio-Sol, over the entire

Bill of materials

Athearn
4700 GP40-2, undec.
42009 truck sideframes
42200 GP35 shell

Detail Associates
1301 cab sunshades
1402 drop steps
1503 m.u. stands
1508 m.u. hoses
1803 antenna
2202 grab irons
2206 lift rings
2504 .012" brass wire
3101 fuel gauges
6206 air hoses
6503 curved grab iron

Details West
126 beacon
139 air filters
152 bell
155 plow
166 fuel fillers

Evergreen styrene
4505 .040" tile sheet, 1/4" squares
9010 .010" plain sheet

Floquil paint
110009 Primer
110010 Engine Black
110013 Grimy Black
110017 Weathered Black
110020 Caboose Red
110040 Dark Green
110070 Roof Brown
110101 Bright Silver

Herald King decals
L-22 CNW early hood units
L-24 CNW hood units
L-25 CNW hood units

Run 8 Productions
1851 cab windows

Scalecoat paint
11 White
35 CNW Green
36 CNW Yellow

Testor Corp.
1160 Dullcote

Mike Danneman

A Chicago & North Western GP40 painted in Pentone Yellow leads a sister unit painted in the traditional yellow scheme out of Milwaukee's Butler Yard in December 1986.

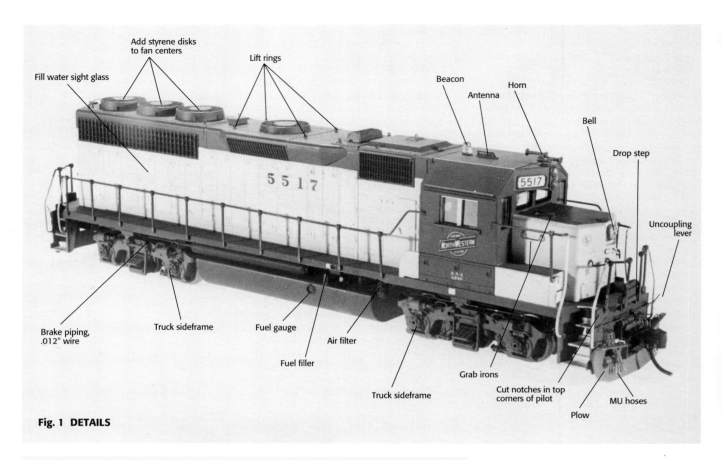

Fig. 1 DETAILS

- Add styrene disks to fan centers
- Fill water sight glass
- Lift rings
- Beacon
- Antenna
- Horn
- Bell
- Drop step
- 5517
- 5517
- Uncoupling lever
- Brake piping, .012" wire
- Truck sideframe
- Fuel gauge
- Air filter
- Fuel filler
- Grab irons
- Cut notches in top corners of pilot
- Truck sideframe
- MU hoses
- Plow

Fig. 2 CAB MODIFICATIONS

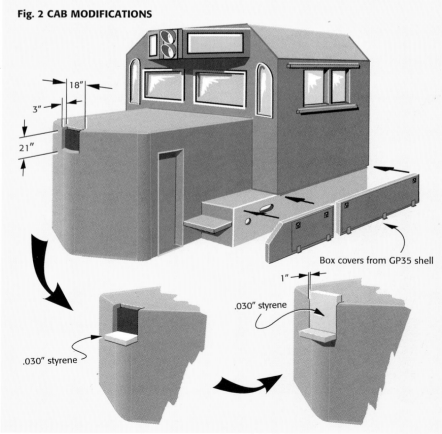

18"
3"
21"

Box covers from GP35 shell

.030" styrene

1"

.030" styrene

shell. This gray makes an excellent base for the bright yellow. I've never had any compatibility problems with the two brands of paint as long as I let the Primer dry for about a week.

Then I painted the shell with the yellow mixture, using about 15 percent Scalecoat thinner. After letting everything dry for another week, I masked the shell with Scotch Magic Transparent Tape. I painted the proper areas CNW Green (thinned as before) and removed the tape.

I used a brush to touch up areas that needed it, then added the handrails. I brush-painted these with Floquil Dark Green, as it covers the metal railings and stanchions much better than Scalecoat. The color difference isn't noticeable. I also brushed some Dark Green around the truck journals.

Next, I brush-painted the smaller details. The pilot steps are painted entirely white, while the remaining steps have white front edges. The handrails and number boards are also white. The fuel filler cap, fuel gauge, emergency fuel cutoff, and front of the m.u. receptacles are red.

The air reservoirs, truck sideframes, window and numberboard gaskets, and air filters are black. I added the bell and left it in its natural metal color. I painted the class lights silver and the grab irons Dark Green. Then I added the rotary beacon, couplers, and hoses.

Decals

I used several different decal sets to obtain all the proper decals. Herald King L-22 provided the hood numerals, which are slightly larger than those found in set L-24. Set L-24 has the properly shaped number board numerals and "CNW" initials for the front and rear hood. Set L-25 provided the "GP40" beneath the cab and the proper cab herald. I also added some small white rectangles on the hood doors to represent stencils on the prototype that mark the locations of the fire extinguisher and other equipment.

Scalecoat is an excellent base for decals. After cutting the decals into the pieces I needed, I positioned them with water and let them set for several minutes. I then brushed some Dio-Sol around the edges. This makes a good bond to the paint. Be careful not to touch the decals until the Dio-Sol is completely dry or they'll be ruined.

After letting the decals dry for several days, I sprayed the body with Dullcote.

Weathering

I weathered the under frame, trucks, fuel tank, couplers, and pilots with a mix of 2 parts Floquil Roof Brown, 2 parts Weathered Black, and 1 part Primer, thinning 1 part of this mixture with 10 parts Dio-Sol. Using an airbrush, I slowly built up coats of the mix to the level I wanted. I used the same solution on the top of the walkways to create a used and dirty look, then gave the entire model a light coat.

For the roof I used Floquil Grimy Black (thinned with 10 parts Dio-Sol). I began around the exhaust stack and worked forward and back, feathering it out and extending it slightly around the sides of the long hood. I also gave the tops of the fans a good coat of this mix.

I used a medium brush to flow some of the black mix into the intake grills on the sides of the long hood. Capillary action pulled this thinned paint into all the crevices and gave the grills some depth. Next, I painted the inside of the exhaust stack Engine Black.

Final details

For the front and rear windows I used vacuformed windows from Run 8 Productions. These windows fit flush with the cab walls, a very nice touch. When trying to install them according to the instructions, I found that the group of four front windows wouldn't sit properly, so I cut them into individual pieces and popped them in. I used .005" clear styrene for the side windows.

Touch up paint that has chipped off, snap the shell to the underframe, and your GP40 is done. My model may not be 100 percent accurate, but it captures the look of the prototype very well.

Modeling Southern Pacific PAs

The author's HO scale Southern Pacific PA-2 no. 6019 leads train no. 101, the *City of San Francisco*. The inset plow gives SP PAs a unique look.

Re-creating famous SP passenger diesels in HO scale

BY BOB FINGERLE

Perhaps none of the Alco PA passenger diesels were as beloved by railfans as those owned by the Southern Pacific. From 1948 to 1967 they pulled such name passenger trains as the *City of San Francisco*, *Shasta Daylight*, *Coast Daylight*, *Golden State*, and the *San Joaquin Daylight*.

The Southern Pacific operated the largest fleet of PAs, buying 53 A units (nos. 6005-6016, 6019-6045, 6055-6068) and 13 B units (5910-5915, 5918-5924) between 1948 and 1953. These took over passenger service from the 4-8-4 *Daylight* steam locomotives and initiated service on the *Shasta Daylight* run.

I chose to model an A-B-A set of early-1950s units. I like the clean lines of the original locomotives, but I wanted to include the snowplow since that was a unique Espee characteristic. I was happy to find data on a set that had some historic significance. In Jan-

uary 1952, PA-1 6013, PB-1 5911, and PA-2 6019 were heading the *City of San Francisco* over Donner Pass when they were stranded for several days near Yuba Gap by a record snowfall – the only passenger train ever to be stopped by snow over Donner Pass. These are the three locomotives that I chose to model.

Modeling

In mid-1990 Athearn rereleased its Alco PA and PB. These are fine models with an upgraded drive system and new truck sideframes. The models are basically a PA-1 and PB-1 as originally delivered by Alco. The PA-2 is identical externally. I started with the undecorated versions.

Begin by removing the cast vertical handrails. I used an X-acto knife for the rough trimming, with masking tape covering all but about 1/8" at the blade

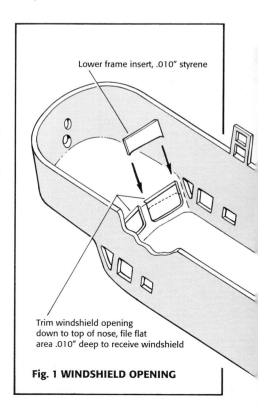

Lower frame insert, .010" styrene

Trim windshield opening down to top of nose, file flat area .010" deep to receive windshield

Fig. 1 WINDSHIELD OPENING

Bob Fingerle

Al Regan; George Drury collection

Striking in its *Daylight* paint scheme, Espee PA-1 no. 6005 pulls the *Shasta Daylight* by Martinez, Calif., in this undated photo.

Use putty to blend lower frame insert with shell

Wipers Drip strip

Access door, .010" styrene, .100" x .115"

Classification lights

6013

Grab iron, .012" wire with nut-bolt-washer castings

Striker, .040" x .080" strip and .020" x .080" strip

Uncoupling lever, .012" wire

Connectors, .010" styrene, .035" x .065", no. 80 holes, drilled .030" apart

Fig. 2 ENGINE FRONT

tip so I wouldn't make any accidental cuts. Be careful not to trim off the handrail end bracket details. You'll need to have a slightly raised trim strip where the door handrails were, but the short rails on the back of the A unit and on both ends of the B unit should be shaved off completely. Sand off all the door handles, as we'll add some wire ones later.

There's some mold flash that must be trimmed on the front of the A unit and on the headlight grillwork. The sides of the grill just to the outside of the horizontal bars should be vertical and crisp. If your shell includes mounting holes for the number boxes, fill them with body putty and sand the areas smooth. Several small molded details on the forward sides also need to be removed, as well as the rivet strips that form the square number boxes on the lower sides near the center cab door (refer to the photos of the finished models).

Windshields and roofline

Trim the bottom of the windshield openings flush with the top of the

nose. Then, as shown in fig. 1, file a flat area on the inside of the lower windshield frame. Since the windshield angle is dependent upon the angle of the filed area, it must be parallel with the front plane of the windshield frame. Cement the lower frame insert in place. Use putty to fill the joints between the frame insert and the shell. Figure 2 shows how the area looks when it's finished.

The Athearn roofline dives down too quickly in front and has an incorrectly shaped drip strip over the windshield. Sand the front faces of the windshield openings flat to knock off the protruding front edge of the top drip strip, using figs. 2 and 3 as guides. Then, using the top edge of the modified windshield opening as a guide, sand the top of the drip strip down to leave the roof edge .045" above the windshield opening. Apply several layers of putty on the roof in front of the dynamic brakes, covering the horn holes. Sand the putty until the roofline matches the contour shown in fig. 3.

Cut a new drip strip as in fig. 3. Cut the strip slightly larger than the template

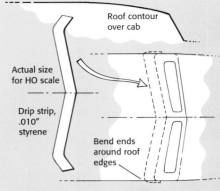

Fig. 3 UPPER CAB AND ROOF DETAILS

so you can make adjustments for the roof contour. The ends should be the same width and approach the roof at the same angle as the side windshield pillars. Be sure the bottom edge of the strip is clearly defined when viewing the locomotive from the front.

Snowplows

The Espee's early PAs, such as no. 6013, had the front of their pilots cut away to make room for the plow. The aft section of the pilot, with its curved cutout around the trucks, was retained as shown in fig. 4. Later units, such as no. 6019, had their pilots completely removed, and units from no. 6022 on were delivered without pilots. This required the railroad to add fabricated support brackets behind the plow.

The plow requires accurate assembly. Its many curves and angles must come together correctly to make it all work. Cut off the Athearn pilot flush with the body sill above the trucks. Make sure that a straightedge placed across the cut is square with the sides of the body.

The PA has a heavy anticlimber above the plow. Build this with .080" styrene. Cut it to match the curve of

the nose and mount it as shown in fig. 5. The location of the back of this part is critical since the plow brackets mount flush with the back. The anticlimber should be flush with the body sides but appear as a separate piece. As it curves toward the front, it should gradually start protruding from the front of the locomotive until it protrudes .010" at the center.

Cut the plow top sheet using the template in fig. 4 as a guide. Be generous when cutting the sweptback sides of the top sheet since they need to intersect with the back corners of the anticlimber. Before gluing, test-fit the top sheet to the anticlimber. When it is centered and its back edge is flush with the back of the anticlimber, the top sheet's long front edges should be flush with the curve of the anticlimber about a third of the way from the center line to the side of the body. Once it fits, cement the top sheet in place and clean up the sides.

Front coupler

The plow surrounds the coupler's draft-gear box while still allowing the coupler to be removed. Modify the Kadee no. 5 draft-gear box as shown in

fig. 6. This allows the plow cutout to be as small as possible. Cut the styrene spacer as shown, then drill a no. 50 hole through both the spacer and anticlimber for a 2-56 screw as shown in fig. 5. Test-mount the coupler to make sure it clears the bottom of the anticlimber, then glue the spacer in place.

Completing the plow

Cut two inner brackets and cement them flush with the back of the top sheet next to the coupler spacer as fig. 5 shows. Make sure that when the front edges of the top sheet are beveled for the plow, the bevel will be continuous with the curve of the inner brackets. Sight down the front edge to do this. Cut two outer plow brackets and glue them to the back corners of the top sheet. Make sure the brackets are parallel to the body sides.

Once the glue has dried, bevel all the brackets for the plow, along with the front of the top sheet. The bevel of the top sheet edge must meet the outer bracket curve. The angled front edges of the top sheet should be beveled completely, but the straight center section can be left alone.

The plow template in fig. 5 includes

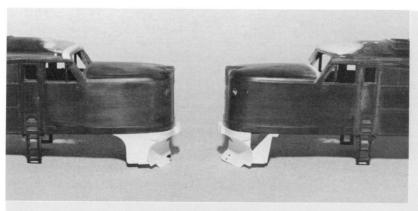

Fig. 4. PLOWS. At left, no. 6013 wears the rear of a standard pilot behind the plow. Number 6019, at right, has a fabricated plow support bracket.

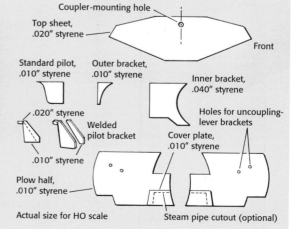

a cutout for access to the steam line connection. A lead unit normally would have the cover shown in the template fitted over the cutout, while a trailing A unit would have the cover removed to make the steam connection with the rest of the train.

If your A unit will be used in both positions, you'll probably want to install the cover since it will only be seen on the front. Both versions can be seen in fig. 4.

I used nut-bolt-washer castings to model the fasteners. The fasteners appear to have been left in place when the cover was removed. When you're building the cover, be sure to curve it to match the curve of the plow.

Cut one plow half as shown in fig. 4, leaving some extra material on the bottom and side edges so the plow can be trimmed to size. Drill the mounting holes for the uncoupling lever brackets. I bent my plow around a ³/₈" dowel, then carefully rolled it around a .200" rod to get its shape close to the curve of the brackets.

Install the draft-gear box when test-fitting the plow to ensure that it can be removed in pieces from behind (the coupler itself comes out the front). The plow's top edge should cover the front of the top sheet. When properly fitted, the top and bottom edges of the plow should be parallel. Check this by eyeballing the fit from the front as well as from below.

Once this piece fits, cement the first half in place and cut out the second. Make the same adjustments to the coupler cutout and check for fit. Trim the inside edges of both halves so they meet on the center line of the locomotive. Once the second half is in place, the final trimming can be done. Make sure that the plow extends beyond the body the same distance on both sides and that the outer edges are vertical when viewed from the front.

For no. 6013's version of the plow support bracket, which was actually the back of the standard pilot, cut two pilot pieces as fig. 4 shows and cement them directly behind the outer plow brackets. For the fabricated bracket,

cut the parts as shown in the template and cement the reinforcement to the front edge of the bracket as shown in the photo.

Detail items

Figure 2 shows how to add the anti-climber front and the front uncoupling levers, which are mounted on the snow-plow. The top lever brackets have the gusset on top, and the lower brackets have the gusset on the bottom. To make the connector between the levers, it's easiest to drill the holes before cutting out the connector. Exact dimensions of the levers varied on the prototype locomotives. The lower lever is one piece across the plow, and the whole assembly is held together with cyanoacrylate adhesive (CA).

I chose to add the small grab irons on the front and rear after painting, but it's wiser to add them first to avoid handling the body after painting. Add the small m.u. receptacle door to the left of the headlight. Form the notch in the door with a no. 80 drill.

Add details to the fuel tank skirts as shown in fig. 7. The battery-charge receptacle is a cover from a Detail Associates m.u. stand set. The fuel filler at the rear must be cut down to fit, and the square hole it mounts in needs to be enlarged slightly. Don't let any of these details stick through the inside, where they can interfere with the chassis and underframe.

Before adding the roof lift rings I squeezed them around .025" wire to correct their shape.

Chassis modifications

The Athearn chassis has lugs over the center of each truck sideframe that help hold the shell in position. The lugs can be trimmed and tapered so they're less visible. Check the horizontal pad on which the trucks pivot and remove any mold flash that would prevent the model from sitting level on the track. The chassis can now be painted Floquil Engine Black.

I mounted Kadee no. 5 couplers on the underframe at the rear of the A units and both ends of the B unit as

Bill of materials

A-Line
29200 windshield wipers

Athearn
3301 PA-1 undec.
3361 PB-1 undec., unpowered

Detail Associates
1106 lift rings
1507 m.u. receptacles
1508 m.u. hoses
1708 classification lights
2203 nut-bolt-washer castings
2213 uncoupling lever brackets
6603 ladder grabs

Details West
167 fuel fillers
174 air horns

Evergreen styrene
124 .020" x .080" strip
144 .040" x .080" strip
155 .060" x .100" strip
9006 .010" clear sheet
9010 .010" sheet
9020 .020" sheet
9040 .040" sheet
9080 .080" sheet

Floquil paint
110010 Engine Black
110015 Flat Finish
110134 SP *Daylight* Orange
110135 SP *Daylight* Red

Kadee
5 couplers

Microscale
87-48 diesel locomotive data decals
87-50 SP *Daylight* diesel decals
MI-1 Micro Set

MV Products
L512 headlight lens set

Utah Pacific
61 speed recorder

Wm. K. Walthers
904-470 Solvaset
933-977 diaphragms

Miscellaneous
clear styrene
.012" wire
.015" music wire

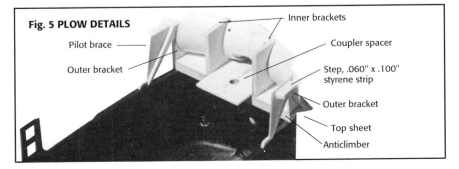

Fig. 5 PLOW DETAILS

Inner brackets
Pilot brace
Outer bracket
Coupler spacer
Step, .060" x .100" styrene strip
Outer bracket
Top sheet
Anticlimber

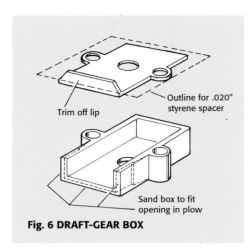

Fig. 6 DRAFT-GEAR BOX

Trim off lip

Outline for .020"
styrene spacer

Sand box to fit
opening in plow

shown in fig. 8. Drill a no. 50 hole .130" from the end of the chassis and tap it for a 2-56 screw. This position gives proper spacing between units and allows use of Walthers rubber diaphragms on the ends. I cut off the Kadee uncoupling pins on my models, which improves the appearance of the front of the lead unit.

Trim the draft-gear boxes off the trucks. The A-unit front presents no particular problem, but in order to clear the other couplers the mounting lugs must be trimmed off the trucks as shown in fig. 8.

Painting

I used Floquil *Daylight* Orange and *Daylight* Red on my models, starting with the red. Use the template in fig. 9 for the orange band – it's best to transfer this pattern to a thin styrene sheet. Prepare the masks by lightly placing 3M Fineline tape on a styrene sheet. Trim the tape using the template, then place the tape on the model. Use the template to locate the bottom edge of the orange band above the anticlimber. The top of the orange band should run just below the batten strip behind the cab and along the bottom of the side air intake screen. The bottom of the orange should split the lower batten strip in the center of the body. Paint the number boxes orange as well.

After you've sprayed the orange, mask the sides and front of the roof and spray it with Floquil Engine Black. Figure 3 shows the pattern of the black

area. After painting, remove all the masking tape and lightly sand the edges of the orange band in front of the cab door with 600-grit sandpaper so the edge doesn't show through the decal stripes. Be careful to touch only the very edge with the sandpaper. Do the same with the red/black division over the top of the cab.

I used Floquil Flat Finish to prepare the model for decals. It has enough of a sheen to allow the decals to sit down properly and doesn't cover fine detail.

Decals

Start with the straight striping on the top or bottom of the body. Use a sharp knife blade to trim the stripes as close as possible to the color to eliminate unwanted decal film. Position the decals using water only and adjust them so they're straight. A coat of Micro Set will soften the stripes and make them easier to adjust. Let them dry to the point where they'll no longer move, then apply Walthers Solvaset very sparingly to set the decal tightly on the body. Don't try to make any adjustments to the decal once you've

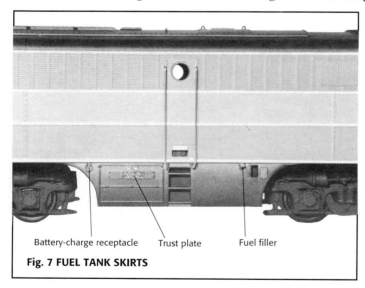

Battery-charge receptacle   Trust plate   Fuel filler

Fig. 7 FUEL TANK SKIRTS

Fig. 8. COUPLERS. Mount Kadee no. 5 couplers on the frame.

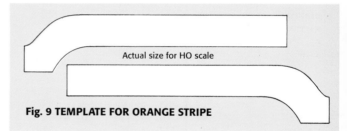

Actual size for HO scale

Fig. 9 TEMPLATE FOR ORANGE STRIPE

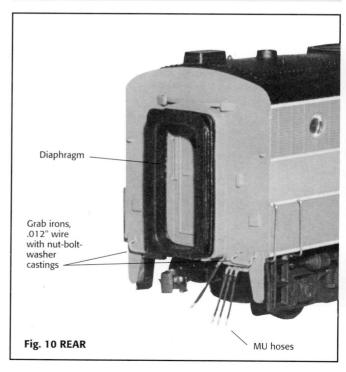

Diaphragm

Grab irons, .012" wire with nut-bolt-washer castings

Fig. 10 REAR

MU hoses

Southern Pacific Lines

John C. Illman

Two years before being stranded in a blizzard at Donner Pass, PA-1 no. 6013 is in charge of the *Cascade* in West Oakland, Calif., in March 1950. Espee PBs wore only a number on the rear half of their sides, with a small "F" placed just above the frame and behind the front handrail.

applied the Solvaset. Apply more light coats of Solvaset as required to set the stripes over rivets. Once they have dried, you may need to lightly touch the stripes with a knife in some places to remove air bubbles.

Carefully cut the curved stripes from the larger orange band decals and use them on the front of the A unit. The curve isn't exactly the right shape, but a little Micro Set softens the stripes so they can be adjusted easily. Let them dry in position even if they have some wrinkles in them.

Now apply the Solvaset and quickly make any adjustments to the shape before the Solvaset softens the decals too much. Use the model and prototype photos as a guide for applying stripes to the plow.

Use the mid-sized numbers on the Microscale no. 87-50 decal sheet for the side numbers. I added trust plates from Microscale set no. 87-48 to the tank skirts, as shown in fig. 7. The "F" on the *Daylight* decal sheet is a bit too large for units with the original paint job, so I used the white letters from the 87-48 set.

The prototype PAs were kept very clean during most of the time they wore the *Daylight* scheme. If you weather your locomotive, I'd suggest concentrating earth tones on the trucks and black on the grills and vents near the roof. Once you've finished the weathering, apply a final coat of Flat Finish to seal the decals.

Final details

Add the Athearn number boxes with their mounting lugs trimmed off, using a small dot of slow-setting CA to mount them. Paint the number board faces black and add a white decal background directly behind the numbers. The Espee placed train numbers in the number boards. A few of the trains that were often pulled by PAs included nos. 9 and 10, the *Shasta Daylight*; 11 and 12, the *Cascade*; 27 and 28, the *San Francisco Overland*; 51 and 52, the *San Joaquin Daylight*; 75 and 76, the *Lark*; and 101 and 102, the *City of San Francisco*. Mount lenses for the classification lights above the number boards as shown in fig. 2.

I modeled the early single headlights by filing a small flat area on the back of each lens and drilling a hole in the center of it to simulate the bulb. Use a no. 60 bit for the small lower light and a no. 55 bit for the top. Slightly enlarge and taper the headlight holes in the body so the lenses are inset; use fig. 2 as a guide. Touch up inside the holes with red paint, then glue the lenses from behind with drops of CA.

Make the vertical handrails out of .015" music wire polished with 600-grit sandpaper. Drill holes for the handrails and bend the wire to fit. Trim all the wires extending inside the shell where they might interfere with the chassis. Form the door handles from .012" brass wire and use a brush to dab them with silver paint.

Add the windshields, using .010" clear styrene. The sides and upper edges must be trimmed very accurately, but this process isn't difficult since each windshield can be test-fitted by holding it in place by the bottom edge, which can be trimmed well below the new bottom frame.

Once trimmed, the windshields are set in place .010" (which is the thickness of the lower frame insert) behind the front face of the frame. Use a small touch of cement between the bottom of the "glass" and the lower frame insert to secure the windshield in place. The overall effect is of a clean, flush installation. I cut the windows in the cab doors to fit flush in the openings, and the same should be done with the cab windows.

Windshield wipers were mounted below the windshields on early units, but these were later mounted above. Add the wipers as shown in fig. 2. Add the m.u. hoses, diaphragm, and grab irons to the A-unit rear and both ends of the B unit, as shown in fig. 10.

Your model is now ready to haul some historic "varnish." After nearly 20 years of operation, the last Alco PAs on the Southern Pacific Lines were retired from service and scrapped in September 1967 after pulling train no. 101, the *City of San Francisco,* one last time. Although not a single Espee PA was saved, you can keep a piece of history alive by modeling locomotives that have disappeared forever. ⚙

Working headlights and truck lights make these HO scale Rock Island Geeps fun to run with the lights down low. The engines are shown switching on Don Bredbeck's layout.

Superdetailing Rock Island GP7s

Adding details and a few surprises to Atlas HO models

BY JOE SINDELAR
PHOTOS BY KEITH THOMPSON

AS A ROCK ISLAND modeler, I'm fascinated with the railroad's 112 Electro-Motive GP7s. As the largest class of diesels on the "Rock," GP7s could be seen doing transfer work or switching a yard one day and heading up a crack "Rocket Freight" the very next day.

Here's how I build 1960s-era Rock Island GP7 models in HO starting with an Atlas GP7. Besides all the "normal" details, my models feature working truck lights, "switchable" constant headlights, full cab interiors, "plugable" m.u. cables, and opening cab windows.

BODY WORK

I start each GP7 by removing the body casting from the metal frame and snapping out all the number boards and

headlights. Next, to make room for the cab interior, I remove the section that splices the short hood to the long hood as shown in fig. 1. I like to leave a 1/16" lip on each hood to make a solid joint when I glue the cab and two hoods together.

Before reassembling the body, I shave off the cast-on grab irons and headlights and drill holes in the hoods for new wire-formed grab irons and lift rings. I then glue the body pieces back together.

After the body joints have set overnight, I add the basic detail parts like lift rings, grab irons, and cab awnings. Rock Island GP7s were delivered with canvas awnings, but a number of engines were converted to steel awnings starting in the early 1960s.

Next, I move the Atlas horns from the sides to the tops of the hoods. I fill the horn-mounting holes on the sides with putty and sand them smooth. Some Rock Island Geeps had their single-chime horns replaced in the early '60s by a three-chime Nathan P3 mounted on top of the nose. Look at prototype photos to see which horn to use.

FRAME

I equip my Geeps with a headlight that can be turned on or off to suit its position in a lash-up. I modify the frame so a small single-pole single-throw (SPST) switch can be mounted under the fuel tank. This requires drilling a hole through the fuel tank and installing the switch. See fig. 2.

This is a good time to drill holes through the frame under the cab to accommodate the truck lights over the front truck. The blocks that stick up into

J. David Ingles

Rock Island 1257 shows off the later-style paint scheme applied to many of the railroad's GP7s in the mid-1950s. Note the squared-off 1,200-gallon fuel tank that was added by the Rock Island.

the cab need to be ground off first. This makes room for the cab interior and means less material to drill through. I use 1.5V microbulbs for the truck lights.

Next, I modify the fuel tank. The original fuel tanks were small, 800-gallon tanks that were almost hidden under the frame. These were soon replaced with 1,200-gallon tanks unique to the Rock Island. The tanks are more or less rectangular, with the bottom edges tapered at about 45 degrees.

To duplicate the prototype tanks, I use sheet styrene to fabricate a new one over the original Atlas tank. I don't have accurate dimensions of the prototype, so I guess at the dimensions using prototype pictures as guides.

The cast-on uncoupling levers on the ends of the frame must be ground off to make room for details like m.u. hoses, drop steps, uncoupling levers, m.u. receptacles, and end grabs.

The flexible handrails that come with the model are too thick for my liking, so I make new ones with .014″-diameter brass wire and 1/2″-high Precision Scale brass stanchions. I add the safety chains that drape between units, and glue small brass wire hooks to the stanchions right of the drop steps. These "catch" the dangling end of another unit's chain.

To the truck sideframes I add a speed recorder and brake cylinder piping, and change the journals to reflect a particular prototype unit. In the early 1960s, the Rock Island's GP7s sported Hyatt roller-bearing, EMD square solid, and EMD slope solid journals with no rhyme or reason for their placement.

PAINT

The Rock Island's GP7s were delivered in a striking red and black scheme with white pinstriping. In the mid-1950s the paint scheme was changed to solid maroon with white pinstriping that closely followed the lines on the original red and black scheme.

The pinstriped maroon scheme was applied to GP7s in two distinct styles. In the first, the nose curl striping came within 2″ of the narrow flat portion of the nose. Many of the GP7s were repainted in this scheme. Also, GP9s 1312-1322 were delivered new in this scheme.

In the later style, the nose curl comes in only halfway on the angled portion of the nose. Some GP7s were repainted, and the remaining GP9s and all GP18s were delivered new in this scheme. Consult prototype photos for correct striping on a particular unit at a specific time.

Using an airbrush, I painted the entire model maroon. There are several shades available on the market, but I prefer Floquil 110160 Rock Island Maroon with a few drops of 110020 Caboose Red and 110011 Reefer White added to give it a slightly reddish tint.

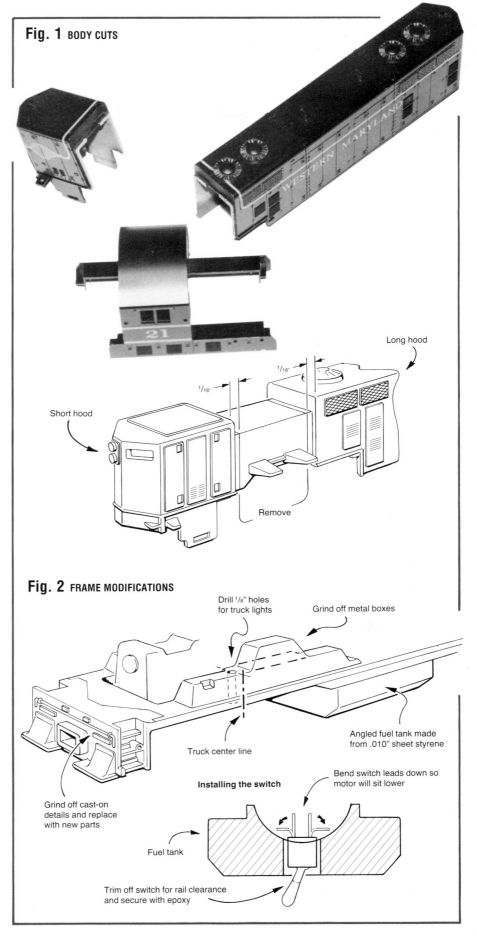

Fig. 1 BODY CUTS

Long hood

Short hood

1/16″

1/16″

Remove

Fig. 2 FRAME MODIFICATIONS

Drill 1/8″ holes for truck lights

Grind off metal boxes

Angled fuel tank made from .010″ sheet styrene

Truck center line

Grind off cast-on details and replace with new parts

Installing the switch

Bend switch leads down so motor will sit lower

Fuel tank

Trim off switch for rail clearance and secure with epoxy

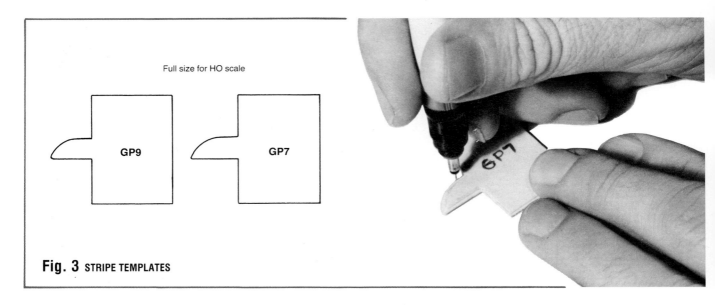

Full size for HO scale

GP9 GP7

Fig. 3 STRIPE TEMPLATES

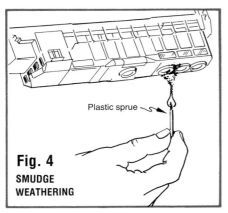

Fig. 4
SMUDGE
WEATHERING

Plastic sprue

Floquil Rock Island Maroon has been discontinued, but may be available at hobby shops. A 10-part Maroon, 3-part Caboose Red, and 1-part Reefer White mix will work. The trucks are painted silver, and some units also had their fuel tanks and air reservoirs painted silver.

Commercial Rock Island decal sets don't have the proper contour for the curl on the nose, so I make my own decal stripes using white ink in a drafting pen and contour templates cut from .020″ plastic sheet. Figure 3 shows the templates for both styles of stripes in HO scale. The templates are a little under-sized to allow for the width of the pen nib.

I cut the straight 2″ striping on the hoods from Microscale white trim film using two single-edge razor blades with a plastic spacer glued between them. The lettering and numbers are from Microscale decal set no. 87-361. The 4″-wide single stripe along the frame is made the same way as the 2″ stripes.

WEATHERING

My way of simulating the exhaust smudge on top of the hoods is rather unorthodox. I hold the model upside down over a piece of burning plastic sprue from a plastic kit. See fig. 4.

WARNING: This technique should only be used outdoors with adequate ventilation. Burning plastic releases harmful chemicals. Avoid breathing the fumes and work quickly.

I move the model briefly back-and-forth over the rising smoke, being careful not to get it too close to the flame. After a couple of passes, I whisk the top off with a soft paintbrush. The result is a realistic and random smudge. Then I spray the entire model with Testor's Dullcote to seal the effect.

For the rest of the weathering I apply washes of Polly S colors. I start with a light wash of Earth over the entire body. The frame receives a wash of Dark Earth followed by a dusting of Grimy Black and a dirt concoction of my own. I spray the exhaust stacks with Engine Black to represent fresh exhaust.

FINISHING TOUCHES

After all the weathering is complete, I reinstall the Atlas cab windows in the ends only. I also add windshield wipers and wind deflectors at this time.

I reinstall the motor using silicone adhesive. The on/off switch in the fuel tank makes the motor sit about $3/16$″ higher, but this doesn't affect the operation of the model.

When rewiring the engine, I make

Fig. 5 WIRING

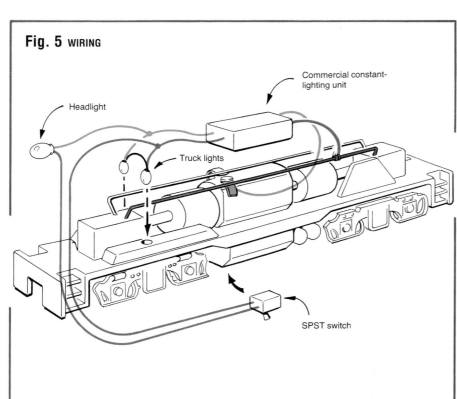

Commercial constant-lighting unit

Headlight

Truck lights

SPST switch

Bill of materials

A-Line
29200 windshield wipers

Atlas
8200 GP7 (no dynamics)

Builders In Scale
250 chain

Detail Associates
1006 dual Mars headlight
1401 drop steps
1507 m.u. receptacles
1508 m.u. air hoses
1708 4½"-diameter class light
1709 7"-diameter class light
2202 grab irons
2205 uncoupling lever
2206 eyebolt
2304 wind deflector set
2805 EMD square journal
2806 EMD slope journal
2807 speed recorder

Details West
164 winterization hatch (for some units)
175 Nathan P3 air horn
188 cab awning

Floquil paint
110011 Reefer White
110020 Caboose Red
110160 Rock Island Maroon

Keystone Locomotive Works
3304 diesel cab interior kit

Microscale
87-361 Rock Island F-unit decals
TF-1 white trim film decal

Polly S paint
410010 Engine Black
410015 Grimy Black
410081 Earth
500076 Dark Earth

Precision Scale
39065 ½" brass stanchions

Radio Shack
275-624 SPST micromini switch

Testor
1260 Dullcote spray

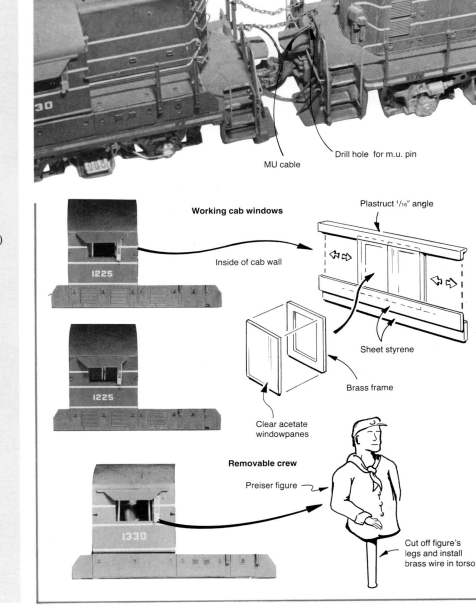

Fig. 6 SPECIAL DETAILS

Multiple-unit connections

Hook for chain

Glue this end of chain to handrail

Drill hole for m.u. pin

MU cable

Working cab windows

Plastruct 1/16" angle

Inside of cab wall

Sheet styrene

Brass frame

Clear acetate windowpanes

Removable crew

Preiser figure

Cut off figure's legs and install brass wire in torso

---

sure that only the headlight wiring is routed through the switch. This way any trailing unit's truck lights stay on all of the time. Figure 5 shows the wiring scheme.

Next, I fabricate and install operating side windows. See fig. 6. I make the window frame from thin brass sheet and attach it to the windowpanes with epoxy. When opening and closing the windows, I use a small, sharp object like a pin to grab the frame.

The cab interior comes next. Only an abbreviated version of the Keystone cab interior can be used because of the drive train. I use the cab seats, control stands, and a portion of the front wall.

I modify the cab seats so that an engineer and a fireman can be seated in the lead unit of a lash-up. I drill small holes in the seats to accept a corresponding pin in the figure's torso. I like to use Preiser figures to represent several crews. I select them based on what their upper body is doing and ignore their legs.

Finally, I fabricate removable m.u. cables from a length of insulation off

the wires of a microbulb. I glue a pin in each end of the cable and insert it into a small hole drilled in each m.u. receptacle. This cable and the chain on the handrails are connected only when the engine is in a multiunit consist.

A lash-up of several Geeps modified this way is truly an impressive sight. The lead unit can have an engineer and fireman, illuminated headlights, number boards, and truck lights, while the trailing units have only illuminated truck lights. All that's missing are the exhaust and the throb of diesel engines. ✿

Amtrak standard power

HO scale F40PH diesels
that look right
and run smoothly

A pair of spanking clean F40PHs leads an excursion at Parker, Ariz., in 1985. You can see how the fuel tank position changed between early units, such as the 214, and those produced later, like the 233.

FOR SOME TIME, I've wanted to add passenger service to my HO scale Ohio Southern RR. What I had in mind was a short train pulled by a single unit, like the Amtrak *Missouri Mule* I watched pulling out of St. Louis with two Amfleet cars behind an F40PH. This looked like the perfect prototype for a layout set in the 1980s. Amfleet cars are available from both Bachmann and Walthers, but the locomotive used to be a big problem.

Several versions of Amtrak's chunky F40PH locomotives have been made in HO, but I wasn't satisfied with their performance. The key to modeling these diesels turned out to be using the Proto Power West no. 53402 F40PH chassis. The units you see here started with Proto Power West mechanisms and undecorated Life-Like body shells, which are available from Wm. K. Walthers as part no. 433-8262. I added a few details and painted them in Amtrak's most recent scheme. Drawings and additional photos of the prototype were published in the April 1987 MODEL RAILROADER.

BODY AND DETAILING

Start by mounting the Life-Like body on the Proto Power West chassis. You'll need to cement blocks of styrene inside the shell to support it at the right height on the frame. The chassis instruction sheet explains the whole procedure, which I covered in a review of the chassis in the March 1988 MR. Put screws through the frame and into the styrene blocks to hold the body securely on the chassis.

While doing the frame installation I decided to make my units models of Amtrak's early or Phase I F40PHs, nos. 200-229. These units have their fuel tanks mounted toward the rear, behind the battery boxes and air reservoirs. That let me retain the left-side engine room steps of the Life-Like bodies, as shown in fig. 1. The later units, with their fuel tanks forward, have step treads set into the tank itself and so are a little harder to model.

Next, I removed the original cast snowplow from the front of the body and built styrene mounting pads for the couplers. Then I added a flat plate of .040" styrene across each end to fill the gaps around the original coupler openings. As you can see in fig. 2, I left just enough room to slide the Kadee no. 5 draft-gear

boxes into place and secured them with 2-56 screws. Adding Details West no. 120 snowplows and Detail Associates no. 1507 m.u. receptacles below the end sills — fig. 3 shows these on the rear of the unit — completed the body work.

PAINT AND DECALS

My Amtrak units are painted with Floquil sprayed directly onto the undecorated body shells. This requires that you adjust the paint volume of your airbrush and your spraying distance so the paint dries almost on contact. The paint has to be a little wet on contact, or you'll get a rough, sandy-looking surface. However, it shouldn't be so wet that it has time to damage the plastic before it dries. I sprayed the black areas first with no. 110010 Engine Black, then let the bodies dry overnight.

Next, I applied masking tape everywhere that was to remain black. I made sure the tape edges made good contact around the details because the silver will leave a mess if it blows under the tape.

r the same reason, I carefully masked
side the windows and portholes. Then I
rayed a light line of black along the
ges of the tape to seal any small leaks
fore applying the silver.

The silver is no. 110144 Platinum
st, and it must be mixed thoroughly
st before spraying because the heavy
etallic pigment settles out rapidly. I
rayed one body, then mixed the paint
ain just to be sure. After waiting
out 20 minutes to give the paint time
set, I removed the masking tape and
t the bodies aside to dry. The next day
sprayed them with clear gloss, then
ve them about a week to dry until
ey no longer smelled of paint solvent.

Microscale decal set no. 87-424 has the
ripes and lettering for the latest Amtrak
heme. The trick is to get the stripes on
raight and level all the way around
ch unit. Figure 4 shows how I used a
akeshift surface gauge to lightly mark
e bottom edge of the blue stripe. To
ke things simpler, the surface details
the model match the prototype.

Applying the decal stripes looks much
sier than it really is. I began by trim-
ing the stripes from the decal sheet,
ing a new knife blade to avoid damag-
g the decal film. I used only water, not
cal solvent, to apply each section of
riping and "float" it into alignment.
en I let most of the water evaporate
d applied the solvent without moving
ything. I let each piece of decal dry
fore adding the next.

The angular nose of the F40PH must be
riped in two sections. Start with one
e of the front and apply a piece of decal
ripe slightly longer than necessary. Let
dry, then carefully slit the decal film
ong the angular joints and remove the
cess film — it should lift right off. Fol-
w with an application of decal solvent so
e fresh decal settles into the details.

Apply the stripe on the opposite side of
e nose in the same way, taking care to
off the excess film without disturbing
e previous piece. If the first decal is dry,
e wet one will not adhere to it. When
th are dry, trim any excess from the
adlight and add a little more decal sol-
nt to settle the ragged edges.

The vertical angles at the rear of the
0PH are no problem, and a single
g decal stripe can wrap all the way
und. Once the solvent had dried, I
t the film along the door edges and ap-
ed more solvent. Then I added the
e stripes, making sure they followed
e guidelines to blend into the end sec-
ns. The last decals to go on were the
mbers and road names.

There were a few little flaws in my de-
striping. I wasn't too concerned with
em as the prototypes take quite a
ating, but I did touch up the worst
ts with a small brush and Floquil's
ntrak Red and Blue. [These colors
ve been discontinued; Floquil's no.
0176 ATSF Red and no. 110151 D&H
ue look close. — A. S.] I'd left the
lded grab irons in place, and I lightly
ushed the outer edges of the vertical
bs with Platinum Mist to make them
nd out. Then I sprayed the bodies
th no. 110015 Flat Finish to hide the
n edges and seal the decals.

Fig. 1. Proto Power West's F40PH chassis comes
with plastic moldings for both the reservoir ends
shown here and the battery box for the opposite
side. Jim Hediger filed the reservoir casting thinner so it would fit behind the engine room step.

Fig. 2. Blocks of styrene were cemented to the
body and filed to proper coupler mounting height.
Both the front and rear pilots were filled in with
styrene sheet, and a plow was installed in front.

Fig. 3. These m.u. receptacles and hoses provide
just enough detail to make the rear of the unit
look good. Jim chose not to add many delicate
detail parts that might be damaged in operation.

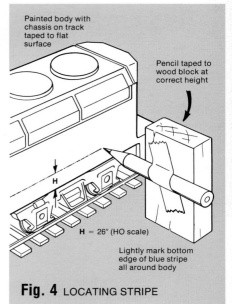

Painted body with
chassis on track
taped to flat
surface

Pencil taped to
wood block at
correct height

H

H = 26" (HO scale)

Lightly mark bottom
edge of blue stripe
all around body

Fig. 4 LOCATING STRIPE

THAT GRIMY LOOK

At this point, I added the m.u. hoses
at the rear and reassembled the units,
but they didn't look quite right. A quick
look at one of the prototypes on my way
to work the next morning showed why.
Seen up close, the real engine was covered with a film of blackish grime. Since
this unit had just come in from Chicago,
where Amtrak does clean its locomotives, this coat of grime evidently doesn't
wash away easily.

That evening, I started weathering my
Amtrak engines by spraying some Floquil no. 110006 Dust and 110083 Mud
onto the running gear and the intake
grills along the top of each side. I also
sprayed some no. 110013 Grimy Black
along the top of the roof on either side of
the silencer hatch to represent the car-
bon deposits from the exhaust. There
wasn't much change until I backed off
and gave the whole unit a light overspray of Grimy Black. The effect was
amazing! That little bit of black turned
the bright Platinum Mist into the perfect shade of grayish silver. I've since
used the same overspray on my Amfleet
cars with similarly good results.

I was careful to make the weathering
subtle. After all, Amtrak does try to
keep its trains looking good for the trav-
eling public. The effect I wanted was
that of a hard-working, high-mileage locomotive — a perfect description of the
F40PH. Judging from the number of
runs they've already made on the Ohio
Southern, I'd expect nos. 217 and 225 to
join the HO scale "million-mile club" in
just a few years. — *Jim Hediger*

John Edwards' HO scale Seaboard U36B mother units are spliced by a double-ended MATE. The GE-built road slug's name is an acronym for "Motors for Added Tractive Effort."

Seaboard mothers and MATEs

Modeling GE road slug power sets in HO

BY JOHN EDWARDS
MODEL PHOTOS BY A. L. SCHMIDT

IN THE EARLY 1970s the Seaboard Coast Line RR was looking for replacement power for its Bone Valley phosphate lines east of Tampa, Fla. The SCL was purchasing U36Bs from General Electric at the time, and GE proposed the idea of "MATEs" to add to their pulling power. MATE, which stands for *Motors for Added Tractive Effort*, describes a road slug with traction motors but no diesel engine or alternator — it draws current from the mother unit's alternator.

Like its predecessors, the Seaboard Air Line and the Atlantic Coast Line railroads, the SCL was not afraid to try new motive power concepts. SCL ordered 10 MATEs in 1971, nos. 3200-3209, and ordered an additional 15 a year later, nos. 3210-3224. U36Bs 1802-1812 and 1835-1855 were modified during construction to operate with the MATEs. The first 10 MATEs are single-ended and can take power from a mother unit at only one end. Those of the second batch are double-ended and can draw power from a mother unit on either end or, in a third mode of operation, from mothers on both ends.

Scott Hartley

Above left. A U36B mother and a double-ended MATE, along with a U23B, await a call at Seaboard System's Port Sutton, Fla., yard. The 1852 still wears her Seaboard Coast Line number with SBD paint in this December 1984 view, though MATE 5224 has been renumbered. The trailing unit is m.u.'ed with the other two, but cannot supply power to or draw fuel from the MATE.

Left. The front of a single-ended SCL MATE. As this end must couple to a mother, it does not need headlights or number boards. The goose-necked pipe is the fuel oil transfer connection that lets MATEs serve as tenders for their mothers.

Author's collection

Number 5208 is a single-ended MATE, with headlights and number boards at the rear only. John rebuilt both MATEs from Athearn U33Bs, the same models he used for his U36Bs.

MATEs differ from ordinary slugs in three ways: their 65,413 to 67,588 pounds of added tractive effort surpasses that of most slugs, they are designed to operate at road speeds, and they also serve as fuel tenders. Each MATE carries 3250 gallons of fuel that the mother unit can draw on while under way. Because of mergers the GE MATEs have served the SCL, then the SBD, and now the CSX; but these 25 remain the only road slugs constructed by a major builder. The roster on this page includes the SBD renumbering.

I decided to build a set of MATEs after seeing photos of them in the *Diesel Spotter's Guide Update* (Kalmbach Publishing Co.). In 1979 I used Athearn U33Bs to build a double-ended MATE along with two U36Bs. After a trip to Florida in early 1985 that included two days of railfanning in the Tampa area, I found that I "needed" another set. Doesn't everyone need four new diesels once in a while?

The MATEs and their mothers had been repainted in the new Seaboard System scheme and they really looked good. Meanwhile, Athearn had just come out with their well-detailed plastic "Blomberg" or GP truck sideframes, and many new detail parts had come on the market since I built my first set.

I've tried to explain everything that I did, but some of the detailing is tedious and you should feel free to leave off anything that seems too much for you. Also, even if you're not interested in kitbashing you may want to check out the detailing of the SBD U36Bs, which don't always run with MATEs. The bill of materials on page 93 identifies those parts that are used only on U36Bs, and also those that are used only on MATEs.

Mother and MATE roster
U36B mother units*
  SCL 1802-1812, renumbered to
    SBD 5753-5763
  SCL 1835-1855, renumbered to
    SBD 5785-5805
Single-ended MATEs
  SCL 3200-3209, renumbered to
    SBD 5200-5209
Double-ended MATEs
  SCL 3210-3224, renumbered to
    SBD 5210-5224

* SCL's U36B fleet included engines 1748 through 1855, but 1801 and 1814 were wrecked and retired. SBD renumbered these units 5700 through 5805, with numbers 5706 and 5720 vacant.

Both author's collection

Above and below. The right and left sides, respectively, of double-ended MATEs. Single-ended versions lack lights and number boards in front and fuel and power connections at the rear, but are otherwise identical. Both units here have SCL numbers, even though no. 3223 has been repainted.

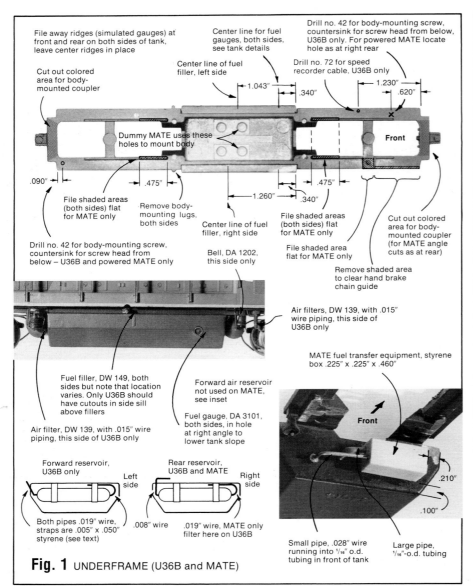

File away ridges (simulated gauges) at front and rear on both sides of tank, leave center ridges in place

Cut out colored area for body-mounted coupler

Center line for fuel gauges, both sides, see tank details

Center line of fuel filler, left side

Drill no. 42 for body-mounting screw, countersink for screw head from below, U36B only. For powered MATE locate hole as at right rear

Drill no. 72 for speed recorder cable, U36B only

Dummy MATE uses these holes to mount body

Front

File shaded areas (both sides) flat for MATE only

Remove body-mounting lugs, both sides

Center line of fuel filler, right side

File shaded areas (both sides) flat for MATE only

File shaded area flat for MATE only

Cut out colored area for body-mounted coupler (for MATE angle cuts as at rear)

Remove shaded area to clear hand brake chain guide

Drill no. 42 for body-mounting screw, countersink for screw head from below – U36B and powered MATE only

Bell, DA 1202, this side only

Air filters, DW 139, with .015" wire piping, this side of U36B only

MATE fuel transfer equipment, styrene box .225" x .225" x .460"

Fuel filler, DW 149, both sides but note that location varies. Only U36B should have cutouts in side sill above fillers

Forward air reservoir not used on MATE, see inset

Air filter, DW 139, with .015" wire piping, this side of U36B only

Fuel gauge, DA 3101, both sides, in hole at right angle to lower tank slope

Forward reservoir, U36B only

Rear reservoir, U36B and MATE

Left side

Right side

Both pipes .019" wire, straps are .005" x .050" styrene (see text)

.008" wire

.019" wire, MATE only filter here on U36B

Front

.210"

.100"

Small pipe, .028" wire running into 1/16" o.d. tubing in front of tank

Large pipe, 1/16"-o.d. tubing

Fig. 1 UNDERFRAME (U36B and MATE)

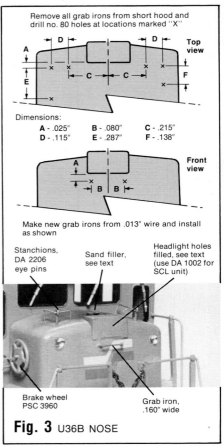

Remove all grab irons from short hood and drill no. 80 holes at locations marked "X"

Top view

Front view

Dimensions:
A - .025" B - .080" C - .215"
D - .115" E - .287" F - .138"

Make new grab irons from .013" wire and install as shown

Stanchions, DA 2206 eye pins

Sand filler, see text

Headlight holes filled, see text (use DA 1002 for SCL unit)

Brake wheel PSC 3960

Grab iron, .160" wide

Fig. 3 U36B NOSE

UNDERFRAMES

Figure 1 shows how to rework the underframes for both the U36B mothers and the MATEs. Before you start, be sure to number the underframes and corresponding body shells and to mark the fronts of the underframes.

I used screws to mount the bodies on my units, eliminating the body mounting lugs and the matching holes in the shells. You won't need to drill screw holes to mount the bodies on unpowered MATEs, as the unused motor mounting holes will suffice. For powered MATEs use the rear mounting screw hole location from fig. 1 at both ends. Test-fit the corresponding bodies when you drill these mounting holes to make sure the screws will come out inside.

The fuel tank details and air-reservoir piping are also covered in fig. 1. Note that each MATE has only one reservoir, behind the fuel tank, so you'll want to remove the front reservoir mounting brackets from the MATE underframes.

I'm not sure why the right fuel filler is farther back than the one on the left, but that's how they are on the Seaboard. Install the air filters per Details West's instructions. (I used .015" wire rather than the .018" they recommend.) On the real locomotive the bell is mounted behind the air reservoir pipe. There isn't room on the model, so I put it between the reservoir pipe and the filter pipe. The bell goes just ahead of the tank on the MATE.

I modeled the diamond-shaped flanges where the pipes enter the ends of the

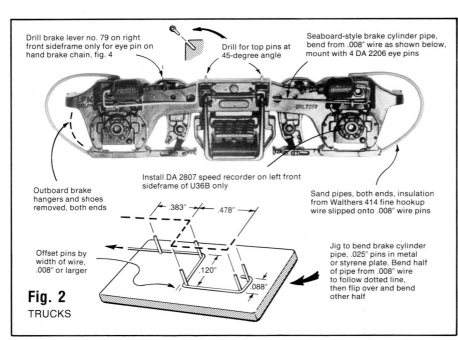

Drill brake lever no. 79 on right front sideframe only for eye pin on hand brake chain, fig. 4

Drill for top pins at 45-degree angle

Seaboard-style brake cylinder pipe, bend from .008" wire as shown below, mount with 4 DA 2206 eye pins

Install DA 2807 speed recorder on left front sideframe of U36B only

Outboard brake hangers and shoes removed, both ends

Offset pins by width of wire, .008" or larger

.383"   .478"

.120"

.088"

Sand pipes, both ends, insulation from Walthers 414 fine hookup wire slipped onto .008" wire pins

Jig to bend brake cylinder pipe, .025" pins in metal or styrene plate. Bend half of pipe from .008" wire to follow dotted line, then flip over and bend other half

Fig. 2
TRUCKS

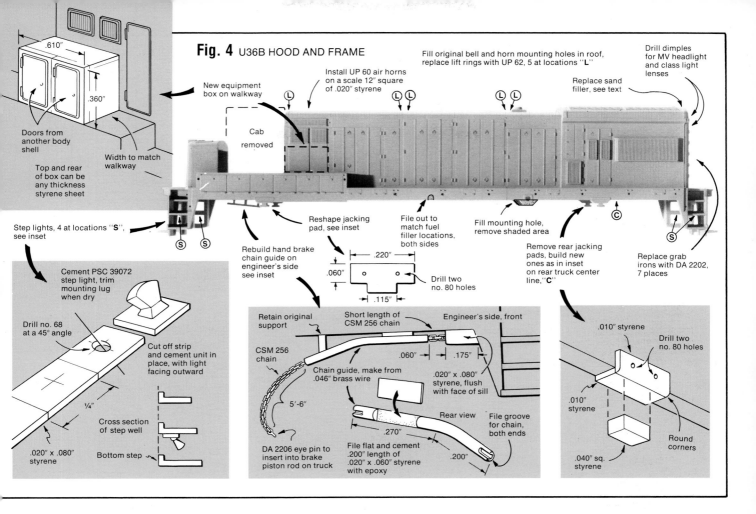

Fig. 4 U36B HOOD AND FRAME

.610"
.360"

Doors from another body shell

Width to match walkway

Top and rear of box can be any thickness styrene sheet

New equipment box on walkway

Cab removed

Install UP 60 air horns on a scale 12" square of .020" styrene

Fill original bell and horn mounting holes in roof, replace lift rings with UP 62, 5 at locations "L"

Drill dimples for MV headlight and class light lenses

Replace sand filler, see text

Step lights, 4 at locations "S", see inset

Reshape jacking pad, see inset

File out to match fuel filler locations, both sides

Fill mounting hole, remove shaded area

Remove rear jacking pads, build new ones as in inset on rear truck center line, "C"

Replace grab irons with DA 2202, 7 places

Rebuild hand brake chain guide on engineer's side see inset

.220"
.060"
.115"

Drill two no. 80 holes

Cement PSC 39072 step light, trim mounting lug when dry

Drill no. 68 at a 45° angle

Cut off strip and cement unit in place, with light facing outward

¼"

Cross section of step well

.020" x .080" styrene

Bottom step

Retain original support

CSM 256 chain

Short length of CSM 256 chain

Chain guide, make from .046" brass wire

5'-6"

DA 2206 eye pin to insert into brake piston rod on truck

File flat and cement .200" length of .020" x .060" styrene with epoxy

.060"   .175"

.020" x .080" styrene, flush with face of sill

Engineer's side, front

Rear view

File groove for chain, both ends

.270"   .200"

.010" styrene

Drill two no. 80 holes

.010" styrene

.040" sq. styrene

Round corners

---

reservoirs with .005" styrene approximately 3" x 6" (HO) and glued these to the ends of the air tanks. I also modeled the reservoir mounting straps by using strips of styrene cut about a scale 4 feet in length. First cement one end of the strap to the underframe mount with cyanoacrylate adhesive (CA), then wrap around the reservoir and cement.

The MATE does have a box in front of its fuel tank that I believe houses the pump for transferring fuel to the mother U36B. Not having a MATE to measure I estimated the dimensions from photos and faked in the fuel lines as shown in fig. 1.

Though it isn't necessary for the models' appearance, I repowered both my U36Bs with Sagami 203239 can motors from NorthWest Short Line, and equipped them with Timewell flywheels. I mounted the motors with silicon sealer, using spacers of scrap styrene strip to hold the motors level while the silicon dried.

TRUCKS

Seaboard U36Bs and MATEs ride on reconditioned EMD trucks from trade-in units, and fig. 2 shows how to remodel and detail the Athearn GP truck sideframes. Assemble the sideframes per Athearn's instructions, but as you do so drill no. 80 holes in the ends of the brake cylinders for the piping and on top of the sideframes for the eye pins that serve as pipe brackets.

The brake-cylinder piping on SCL/SBD U-boats with reconditioned EMD trucks is

different from any other road's that I've seen, and so it is well worth modeling. These pipes aren't easy to bend, though, and .008" wire is very fragile and won't take much re-bending at the same location. I'm not a wizard with wire and for every good pipe I got I had to make three — don't get discouraged!

Four units need 16 pipes, so I built the jig shown in fig. 2 for "mass production." You could use slightly larger wire by adjusting the offset of the second and third pins from the left. Even though I measured, figured, and double-checked, I still had to move some pins to get my air lines to come out right. Once I had the pins located correctly I secured them with CA.

Use the jig to bend half an air line, then flip it over and bend the other half. When you've mastered the technique the air lines will come out at a fairly rapid clip, though they'll still need some final straightening with small pliers. Thread the eye pins onto the air line and install with CA.

U36B HOODS

General Electric U36B and U33B locomotives are outwardly identical, so most of the work on the Athearn U33B body shell involves adding detail and special SCL/SBD features. Start with the short hood as shown in fig. 3. For a Seaboard System unit, it will be easier to apply the nose logo decal if you don't install the small grab under the headlight housing until later.

You may wish to replace the sand filler. I used Detail Associates no. 3001 EMD fillers, but now Details West has the correct GE part, no. 203. For an SBD unit, fill the lower headlight holes with plastic as shown. For an SCL unit, file the front of the headlight housing flat and install a Details West no. 148 headlight.

Next, modify the long hood as shown in fig. 4. For an SCL unit go ahead and install the horn now, but for an SBD leave it off so you can paint it black separately. Note that Athearn's four-axle U-boats all have the rear jacking pad in the wrong place: it should line up with the center of the truck. If you're building a U36B for a different railroad, check prototype photos, as the shape of the jacking pad is not always the same.

Remove the hand brake chain guide on the engineer's side, but leave its rearmost support in place, and make a new chain guide as in the figure. I made it as a subassembly, first cementing the styrene and chain to the wire with five-minute epoxy and then securing it to the body with styrene cement and more epoxy.

The equipment box behind the cab on the fireman's side is a common addition to many roads' U-boats, and it even comes in different sizes. Seaboard System units have the box as shown with two doors, but in SCL times it was half as long and had only one door. Take the doors from another U-boat body as shown — if you're building a MATE, too, the doors can come from one of the bodies you'll use for that.

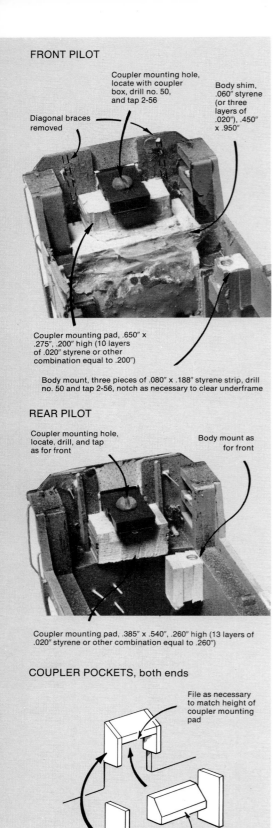

FRONT PILOT

Diagonal braces removed

Coupler mounting hole, locate with coupler box, drill no. 50, and tap 2-56

Body shim, .060" styrene (or three layers of .020"), .450" x .950"

Coupler mounting pad, .650" x .275", .200" high (10 layers of .020" styrene or other combination equal to .200")

Body mount, three pieces of .080" x .188" styrene strip, drill no. 50 and tap 2-56, notch as necessary to clear underframe

REAR PILOT

Coupler mounting hole, locate, drill, and tap as for front

Body mount as for front

Coupler mounting pad, .385" x .540", .260" high (13 layers of .020" styrene or other combination equal to .260")

COUPLER POCKETS, both ends

File as necessary to match height of coupler mounting pad

.080" x .100" styrene, .310" long, with 45-degree bevel filed on one corner as shown

.020" x .080" styrene, 240" long (2), (trim to match bevel of center after assembly)

Fig. 5 U36B BODY AND COUPLER MOUNTS

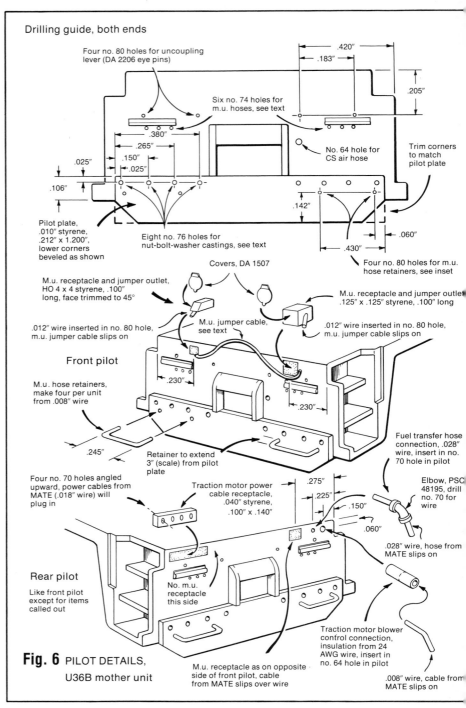

Drilling guide, both ends

Four no. 80 holes for uncoupling lever (DA 2206 eye pins)

Six no. 74 holes for m.u. hoses, see text

.420"

.183"

.205"

.380"

.265"

.150"

.025"

.025"

.106"

Trim corners to match pilot plate

No. 64 hole for CS air hose

.142"

.060"

.430"

Pilot plate, .010" styrene, .212" x 1.200", lower corners beveled as shown

Eight no. 76 holes for nut-bolt-washer castings, see text

Four no. 80 holes for m.u. hose retainers, see inset

Covers, DA 1507

M.u. receptacle and jumper outlet, HO 4 x 4 styrene, .100" long, face trimmed to 45°

M.u. receptacle and jumper outlet .125" x .125" styrene, .100" long

.012" wire inserted in no. 80 hole, m.u. jumper cable slips on

M.u. jumper cable, see text

.012" wire inserted in no. 80 hole, m.u. jumper cable slips on

Front pilot

.230"

.230"

M.u. hose retainers, make four per unit from .008" wire

Fuel transfer hose connection, .028" wire, insert in no. 70 hole in pilot

.245"

Retainer to extend 3" (scale) from pilot plate

Four no. 70 holes angled upward, power cables from MATE (.018" wire) will plug in

Traction motor power cable receptacle, .040" styrene, .100" x .140"

.275"

.225"

.150"

.060"

Elbow, PSC 48195, drill no. 70 for wire

.028" wire, hose from MATE slips on

Rear pilot

Like front pilot except for items called out

No. m.u. receptacle this side

Traction motor blower control connection, insulation from 24 AWG wire, insert in no. 64 hole in pilot

.008" wire, cable from MATE slips on

Fig. 6 PILOT DETAILS, U36B mother unit

M.u. receptacle as on opposite side of front pilot, cable from MATE slips over wire

PILOTS

I removed everything from the pilot faces except the m.u. hose mounting points and the bar just above them. I even removed the angled portion of the porch. The Seaboard System uses 26L braking so only the three inner m.u. hose locations are used. I removed the three inner lugs on each side and drilled no. 74 holes for six Detail Associates m.u. hoses. SCL U36Bs carried only three hoses at each end, generally the three to the left as you face the pilot.

Remove the cast-on stiffeners behind the front pilot and add a shim as shown in fig. 5 to support the front end of the frame at the proper height. (This is not necessary on the MATEs.) Then build both the front- and rear-coupler mounting pads as in the figure. I used plenty of liquid cement and allowed lots of drying time as a strong assembly is required. When you drill the coupler mounting holes, be very careful not to break through the walkway. Check your drill bit frequently and stop at the first sign of black chips.

Strength is also important for the body mounting blocks. Build them as shown in fig. 5, locating and drilling them to match the mounting holes you drilled in the metal underframe. After drilling and tapping the blocks, bore out the underframe

Bill of materials

Athearn
3480 U33B, powered undec., U36B or MATE
3490 U33B, dummy undec., U36B or MATE
34900 U33B body, undec., second body to build MATE
42011 EMD "Blomberg B" power trucks
90459 EMD "Blomberg B" dummy trucks

Cal Scale (CS)
276 air hoses

Campbell Scale Models (CSM)
256 chain

Detail Associates (DA)
1002 headlight, for nose light on SCL U36B only
1202 bell
1301 sunshade, SBD U36B only
1402 drop step
1507 m.u. receptacles, use covers only
1508 m.u. hoses
2202 grab irons, U36B only
2203 nut-bolt-washer (n.b.w.) castings
2205 uncoupling levers, SCL units
2206 eye bolt (eye pin)
2212 uncoupling levers, SBD units
2807 speed recorder, U36B only
3001 EMD sand filler hatch (as used by author)
3101 fuel gauge

Details West (DW)
139 air filter set, U36B only
149 GE fuel filler
157 "firecracker" antenna
203 GE sand filler hatch (preferred to DA 3001)

Evergreen Scale Models (ESM) styrene
101 .010" x .030" strip
103 .010" x .060" strip
123 .020" x .060" strip
124 .020" x .080" strip
142 .040" x .040" strip
165 .080" x .100" strip
168 .080" x .188" strip
186 .125" x .125" strip
8404 HO 4 x 4 strip
8612 HO 6 x 12 strip

Floquil paint
110010 Engine Black
110012 Reefer Gray, SBD only
110015 Flat Finish
110017 Weathered Black
110168 UP Armour Yellow

Grandt Line
5124 freight car ladder, MATE only

Herald King decals
L-380 Seaboard Coast Line hood unit
L-1940 Seaboard System hood unit*.
Deep Yellow Stripes*

Kadee
5 couplers

Microscale decals
87-398 Seaboard System diesel units*

M. V. Products
18 headlight lenses
22 class light lenses

Polly S "Flats" paint
500021 Venetian Dull Red

Precision Scale Co. (PSC)
3909 Alco louvers, MATE only
3960 brake wheel
3968 windshield wipers, U36B only
39072 step lights
48195 elbows

Testor's Military Flat paint
1181 Aluminum

Utah Pacific (UP)
60 air horn, U36B only
62 GE lift rings, U36B only
87 GE handrail stanchions

Wm. K. Walthers
942-414 fine hookup wire

Miscellaneous
.005", .010", .020", and .040" styrene sheet
.008"-, .015"-, .019"-, .028"-, and .046"- dia. brass wire
1/16"-o.d. brass tubing
2-56 screws

* The author used Microscale decals on his U36Bs and Herald King decals on his MATEs. The two brands had slightly different yellows, and he recommends using Herald King decals for all units.

---

oles for screw clearance (³/₃₂" or no. 42) nd countersink to hide the screwheads.

Before mounting the couplers — mine re Kadee no. 5s with the uncoupling pins emoved — I added the coupler pockets hown in fig. 5. They look more prototypi- al than the plain rectangular openings of he stock pilots. Temporarily assemble the odies to the underframes and trucks, hen screw the couplers in place. Check hem with a Kadee coupler height gauge, nake any adjustments necessary, then re- nove the couplers and set them aside.

Figure 6 shows the remaining pilot de- ails, including the special mother unit ower and fuel connections on the rear pi- ot. Initially I installed the nut-bolt- vasher castings as shown, but I later had o cut them off when the decals wouldn't nuggle down over them. If you wish to dd them, drill their holes now, but in- tall and hand paint them only after the lecals have been applied. In fact, this ap- lies to the uncoupling levers, m.u. and rake hoses, and hose retainers as well. The front m.u. jumper cable will be a cale 9-foot length of insulation from Wal- hers no. 414 fine hookup wire, and this oo should be added after painting.

U36B CABS

Figure 7 shows how to rework the Athearn cabs. I filled the original hand- ail holes at this point, but waited to Irill new holes to fit my new handrails.

For SCL units as built, you can leave he four small side windows as they :ome, but these were filled in sometime before the U36Bs were repainted by the

SBD. It appears that on some units the glass was simply painted over, but oth- ers had the openings filled with sheet metal. I used styrene sheet and filler.

Note that the top of the headlight housing on these units is square rather than round. Also, for SBD units only, add Detail Associates no. 1301 sun shades above the windows on each side.

MATE BODIES

It takes two U33B bodies to make one MATE. Cut them as shown in fig. 8 and join the two rear frame sections to make the MATE frame. The reason for making the joint fall *exactly* in the middle of the handrail stanchion hole is to let the stan- chion hide the seam, and this also makes

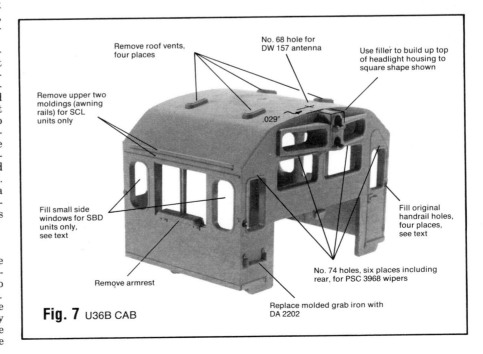

Remove roof vents, four places

No. 68 hole for DW 157 antenna

Use filler to build up top of headlight housing to square shape shown

Remove upper two moldings (awning rails) for SCL units only

.029"

Fill small side windows for SBD units only, see text

Fill original handrail holes, four places, see text

No. 74 holes, six places including rear, for PSC 3968 wipers

Remove armrest

Replace molded grab iron with DA 2202

Fig. 7 U36B CAB

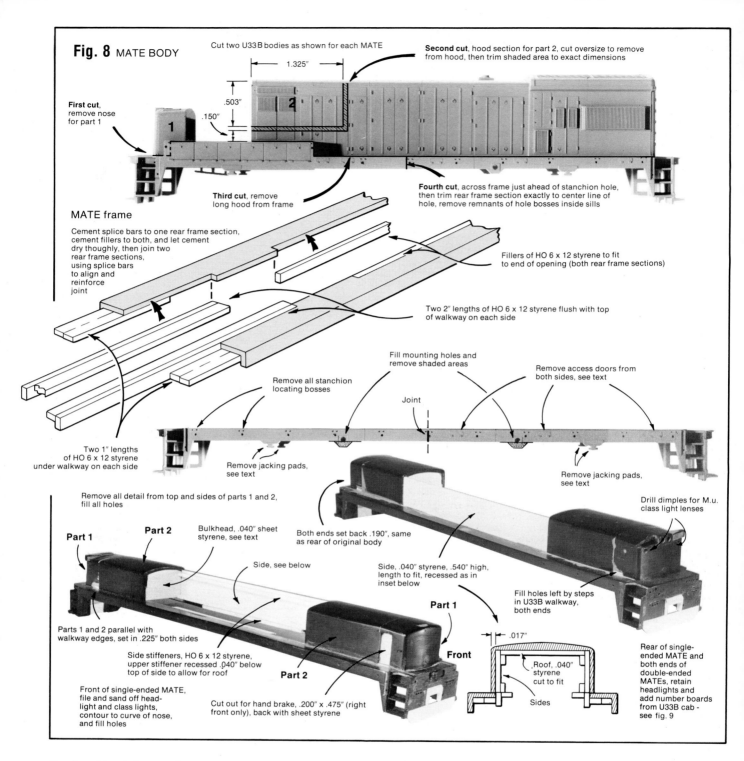

Fig. 8 MATE BODY

Cut two U33B bodies as shown for each MATE

1.325″

.503″

.150″

First cut, remove nose for part 1

1

2

Second cut, hood section for part 2, cut oversize to remove from hood, then trim shaded area to exact dimensions

Third cut, remove long hood from frame

Fourth cut, across frame just ahead of stanchion hole, then trim rear frame section exactly to center line of hole, remove remnants of hole bosses inside sills

MATE frame

Cement splice bars to one rear frame section, cement fillers to both, and let cement dry thoughly, then join two rear frame sections, using splice bars to align and reinforce joint

Fillers of HO 6 x 12 styrene to fit to end of opening (both rear frame sections)

Two 2″ lengths of HO 6 x 12 styrene flush with top of walkway on each side

Two 1″ lengths of HO 6 x 12 styrene under walkway on each side

Remove all stanchion locating bosses

Remove jacking pads, see text

Joint

Fill mounting holes and remove shaded areas

Remove access doors from both sides, see text

Remove jacking pads, see text

Drill dimples for M.u. class light lenses

Remove all detail from top and sides of parts 1 and 2, fill all holes

Part 1

Part 2

Bulkhead, .040″ sheet styrene, see text

Both ends set back .190″, same as rear of original body

Side, see below

Side, .040″ styrene, .540″ high, length to fit, recessed as in inset below

Fill holes left by steps in U33B walkway, both ends

Parts 1 and 2 parallel with walkway edges, set in .225″ both sides

Side stiffeners, HO 6 x 12 styrene, upper stiffener recessed .040″ below top of side to allow for roof

Front of single-ended MATE, file and sand off headlight and class lights, contour to curve of nose, and fill holes

Part 2

Part 1

Front

Cut out for hand brake, .200″ x .475″ (right front only), back with sheet styrene

.017″

Roof, .040″ styrene cut to fit

Sides

Rear of single-ended MATE and both ends of double-ended MATEs, retain headlights and add number boards from U33B cab - see fig. 9

---

the stanchion holes evenly spaced. I used Scotch tape to protect the walkways when cutting the hoods off flush. While you're doing all this cutting, go ahead and remove the pilot detail as for the U36B.

Using two rear frame sections this way, you end up with side sill access doors on both sides, instead of just on the left as on the prototype. After designating one end as the front — the brake wheel goes at the right front — you could remove those on the right and make new ones for the left from .005″ styrene sheet. I just removed all of them from both sides and did without.

Make new jacking pads as shown for the rear of the U36B back in fig. 4. Make sure you locate them on the truck center lines.

When the frame is ready, use the parts from the U33B nose and hood and some styrene sheet and strip to build the MATE hood as shown in fig. 8. Do this with the frame in place on the metal underframe, or the frame may bow upwards in the center. I made a couple of reference marks .225″ in from the edge of the walkways on each side to help get the new hood straight and parallel on the frame.

If you want to build a powered MATE, you'll have to make the bulkheads in the ends of the hood U-shaped to clear the drive shafts from the motor. If your MATE will be a dummy, though, the solid bulkheads are simpler to make. Note that, first, the new center section of the hood must be set in from the wider U33B parts on each side and, second, there's a step down from the ends to the flat roof of the center section. If you choose to keep the access doors on one side sill, be sure they're on the left and that the brakewheel recess is on the opposite side.

You'll need to work on the body mounting before you cement the hood roof in place. Figure 9 shows how I mounted the bodies on my dummy MATEs using two of the motor mounting holes in the fuel tank. With the body on the underframe and the top of the hood open, you can see how to align that topmost styrene plate on the stiffeners and then work down from there. On the underframe work up from the bottom of the fuel tank recess, using CA to bond styrene to metal.

Let the cement harden, then put the body on the underframe and drill no. 50 holes up through the forward motor mount holes. Remove the body, tap its mounting holes 2-56, and open the underframe holes with a no. 42 clearance bit. Then you can secure the body with 2-56 screws. For a powered MATE make mounting blocks and drill the underframe as for the rear of the U36B, fig. 5.

When the body mounting is complete, cement the hood roof in place. Fill and sand all joints in the MATE body before going on. You can also make coupler mounts as for the rear of the U36B, fig. 5, and add the coupler pocket and pilot plate details as in figs. 5 and 6. There's some specialized pilot detailing for the MATEs that I'll cover a little later.

MATE DETAILS

Start detailing the MATE body by adding the number boards from a U33B cab on each side of the headlight as in fig. 10. Notice that for a single-ended MATE these go on the rear end only, but that a double-ender has them at both ends.

Notching the hood ends for the number boards is easier than it looks if you grind off the sides of an X-acto no. 17 blade to make a narrower chisel. Take your time and test-fit the number boards often. Hold the beveled edge of the blade to the inside of the cut and keep the edge sharp. I sharpened my blade on a small Arkansas stone after each couple of cuts so the edge was always "new."

When you're satisfied with the notches, cement the number boards in place. Cut out the center headlight portion of the clear styrene insert and trim the number board inserts to fit. Use filler to square up the backs of the number boards even with the back of the headlight housing.

The side details are the same on both single- and double-ended MATEs, so you can use fig. 11 as a guide for either one. The doors and grills for the left side can come from one of the U33B bodies you cut up. You might notice that the left-side grills on my MATEs are not correctly located — I measured my older model thinking it was correct, and it wasn't! — but the dimensions in fig. 11 will put your grill where it belongs.

On the right side I scribed my own doors, as there are only two suitable doors on each U33B and the right side of the MATE needs five. To simulate the recessed door handles I first indented the spot with a needle, drilled a shallow pilot hole with a no. 68 bit, then started drilling with a no. 52 bit but stopped when the hole reached a diameter comparable to Athearn's cast handles. You may wish to practice this first next to a cast handle on a piece of scrap hood.

Thinning the Precision Scale Alco louvers is easily done on an emery board using one finger to slide the part back and forth. You can tell when you've got the louvers thin enough by holding them to the light. The raised louvers should appear dark against a translucent light brown background.

Again, while I used a Detail Associates EMD sand filler hatch, you'll probably want to use the new GE-style part from Details West.

Pilot details on MATEs come in two flavors. The rear pilot of the single-ended units is like the front pilot of the U36B (see fig. 6), except that it has only one m.u. receptacle, on the right side as you face the pilot. The front pilot of the single-ender and both pilots on a double-ended MATE are similar to the rear pilot of the U36B mother, but the m.u., fuel, and power connections are in mirror image. Figure 12 shows this and lists the cables and hose you'll need to connect a MATE to its mother unit.

The grabs on top of the hoods were installed after the MATEs had seen a few years' service. If you're modeling an early SCL version, you need not bother. For my Seaboard System MATEs I made the template in fig. 13. Make one 90-degree bend on a piece of .008" wire and place it into one of the template's end holes. Lay the wire flat on the template, bend it all the way around to the other end hole, then bend it 90 degrees again. Drill holes in the MATE using the same template.

HANDRAILS

To those of you who can bend a wire handrail once and have it come out right, I doff my hat. For me it's a lot of work and I don't know any secrets. The side railings for the U36B are like Athearn's, but I made new ones from .015" brass wire, which is smaller and closer to scale. When I got the railings bent I threaded on the required number of Utah Pacific stanchions, slipped them into their holes in the frame, and soldered them to the wire — you could use CA as well. After doing that I removed the railing/stanchion subassemblies and set them aside for painting.

The side railings for the MATEs are simple because they're straight, though the stanchion spacing you end up with doesn't match the prototype's. From front to rear the first 8 stanchions are a scale 5'-0" apart, 8 and 9 are 3'-0" apart, 9 and 10 are 5'-5" apart, and 10 and 11 are 5'-6" apart. The rear stanchions on the U36B should follow this spacing too, though I decided to live with the stanchion spacings of the Athearn models.

The end railings for both U36Bs and MATEs are shown in fig. 14 and should be installed permanently before painting. I took the trouble to make them this

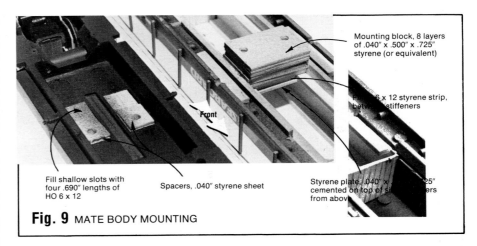

Fill shallow slots with four .690" lengths of HO 6 x 12

Spacers, .040" styrene sheet

Mounting block, 8 layers of .040" x .500" x .725" styrene (or equivalent)

6 x 12 styrene strip, between stiffeners

Front

Styrene plate, .040" x .25" cemented on top of stiffeners from above

Fig. 9 MATE BODY MOUNTING

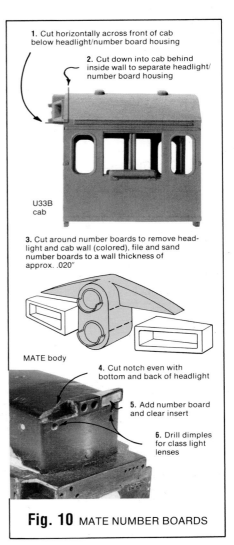

1. Cut horizontally across front of cab below headlight/number board housing

2. Cut down into cab behind inside wall to separate headlight/number board housing

U33B cab

3. Cut around number boards to remove headlight and cab wall (colored), file and sand number boards to a wall thickness of approx. .020"

MATE body

4. Cut notch even with bottom and back of headlight

5. Add number board and clear insert

6. Drill dimples for class light lenses

Fig. 10 MATE NUMBER BOARDS

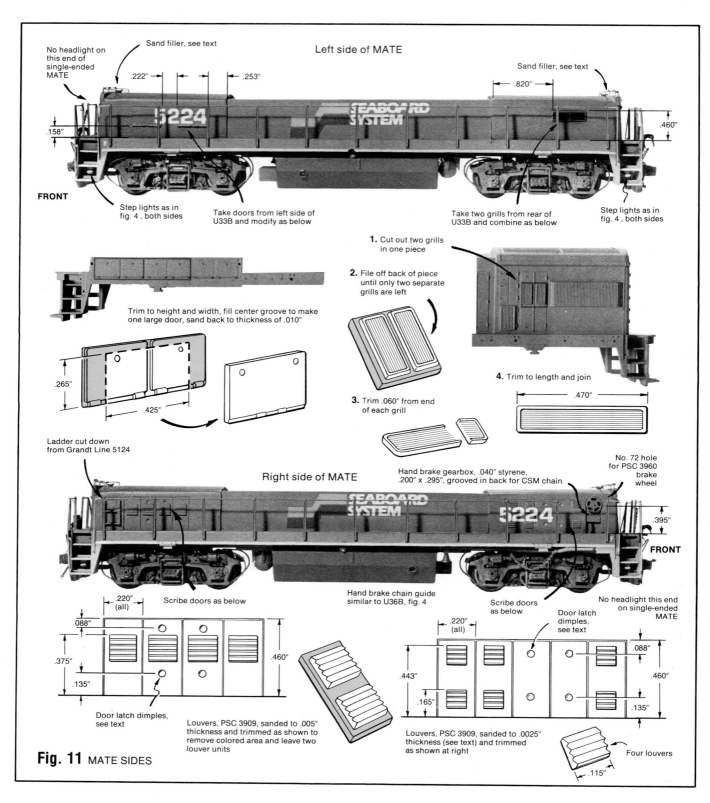

No headlight on this end of single-ended MATE

Sand filler, see text

Left side of MATE

Sand filler, see text

.222″   .253″

.820″

.158″

.460″

FRONT

Step lights as in fig. 4 , both sides

Take doors from left side of U33B and modify as below

Take two grills from rear of U33B and combine as below

Step lights as in fig. 4 , both sides

Trim to height and width, fill center groove to make one large door, sand back to thickness of .010″

1. Cut out two grills in one piece

2. File off back of piece until only two separate grills are left

.265″

.425″

3. Trim .060″ from end of each grill

4. Trim to length and join

.470″

Ladder cut down from Grandt Line 5124

Right side of MATE

Hand brake gearbox, .040″ styrene, .200″ x .295″, grooved in back for CSM chain

No. 72 hole for PSC 3960 brake wheel

.395″

FRONT

No headlight this end on single-ended MATE

Hand brake chain guide similar to U36B, fig. 4

.220″ (all)

Scribe doors as below

Scribe doors as below

Door latch dimples, see text

.088″

.375″

.460″

.135″

.088″

.460″

.135″

.220″ (all)

.443″

.165″

Door latch dimples, see text

Louvers, PSC 3909, sanded to .005″ thickness and trimmed as shown to remove colored area and leave two louver units

Louvers, PSC 3909, sanded to .0025″ thickness (see text) and trimmed as shown at right

Four louvers

.115″

Fig. 11 MATE SIDES

way so the center stanchions would look like the real thing, and to me the results are worth the bother. For four units I needed 16 center stanchions, so I made them assembly-line style:

• Round one end of the styrene strip.
• Use a pin to make dimples for the three holes and drill all three no. 80.
• Check that the holes come out centered and cut the stanchion to length; discard any that aren't right and start again.

Repeat these first three steps until you have all the stanchions you'll need.

• Enlarge the handrail and nut-bolt-washer holes with gradually larger bits. If a hole breaks out the side, discard that stanchion and start again.
• Add the chain hooks and n.b.w. castings. Both go to the *outside* of the stanchion, and you'll need a pair of left and right stanchions for each end.

When the center stanchions are ready,

follow the directions in fig. 14 to install the end railings. Make sure the railings and stanchions are straight and square before cementing with CA. Mine aren't perfect, but compare an Athearn U-boat with stock handrails and the improvement will be obvious.

PAINTING

SBD's locomotives and MATEs are painted "Seaboard French Gray." As

Tom Busack asked in his SD50 modeling article in the January 1984 MODEL RAILROADER, "What is SBD French Gray?" Like him I've found that it appears to be many different shades depending on paint batches, lighting, weathering, and so on. Since no paint manufacturer has come to our aid with a color called SBD French Gray, I tested several different paints on a scrap section of hood. After comparing my samples with every SBD photo I had, I decided that Floquil Reefer Gray is very close.

I sprayed the bodies with a first coat of Reefer Gray and then repaired any areas that needed additional work. You may be surprised to find out how many blemishes stand out clearly in light gray that were well hidden while still black. A second coat of Reefer Gray was allowed to dry, and then I masked off the bodies and painted the pilots Engine Black. This extends to just under the edge of the walkway. On the underframes and trucks I used Weathered Black darkened just a little with Engine Black. Under normal lighting it looks black, but it doesn't hide the detail that a true black does. I gave the couplers and wheelsets a light spray of Floquil Rail Brown.

All grill openings were hand painted with a 50/50 mixture of India ink and rubbing alcohol. The exhaust stacks along with the ends of the m.u. jumper cables, the windshield wipers (except blades), and the side window posts were painted a flat aluminum. The jumper cables themselves were painted Polly S Heritage Red; all other cables were painted Weathered Black, as were the horns. The uncoupling levers are Engine Black, except for the straight, horizontal sections on each side, which are Floquil Armour Yellow.

Apply the decals according to the manufacturer's instructions. When the decals are dry give the units a flat sealer coat. Reinstall the handrails now, along with brake wheels, m.u. hoses, uncoupling levers, horns, and couplers. Paint the vertical ends of the handrails Armour Yellow up to the first stanchion.

My models are meant to represent recently repainted units, so the weathering is light. I mixed nine parts of Floquil Dust with to one part Reefer White, thinned this about 3:1 with Dio-Sol for a very light finish, and sprayed it up from below onto the underframe and trucks. I used black chalk to weather the roof and grill openings.

I cut the number boards to size from .010" white styrene, applied the black decal numerals, and cemented them in place. After another coat of flat to seal the weathering, I installed the M. V. Products lenses in the headlights and classification lights.

Use tweezers to install the cables and hoses on the MATE and secure them with CA. With the units on the track, use tweezers to make the connections to the mother U36B. Couple the units and attach the safety chains between them. You are now ready to haul 10,000-ton phosphate trains on your layout, or at least some load substantial enough to justify all that tractive effort! ✿

Fig. 12 MATE PILOT DETAILS

Front of single-ended unit, both ends of double-ended unit

Traction motor blower control connection, see fig. 6

M.u. receptacle as on front of U36B, see fig. 6

.050" spacing

.275"

.150"

.045"

.145"

.125"

.225"

.020"

Traction motor power cable receptacles, lengths of .030"-dia. wire insulation inserted in no. 68 holes and extending 6 scale inches, cables to mother (.018" wire) will plug in

Fuel transfer pipe

.250"

Elbows, PSC 48195, pushed together with .015" wire connection

.028" wire hose to mother slips on

Cables and hoses for one mother/MATE connection:
1. M.u. jumper cable: 9'-0"(HO) length of .020"-dia. wire insulation, Walthers fine hookup wire
2. Fuel transfer hose: 6'-0" length of .040"-dia. wire insulation
3. Traction motor blower control cable: 7'-0" length of .020"-dia. wire insulation
4. Traction motor power cables: Four 8'-0" (or longer) lengths of .018"-dia. flexible solid wire

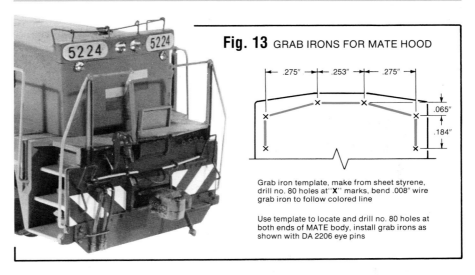

Fig. 13 GRAB IRONS FOR MATE HOOD

.275" .253" .275"

.065"

.184"

Grab iron template, make from sheet styrene, drill no. 80 holes at "X" marks, bend .008" wire grab iron to follow colored line

Use template to locate and drill no. 80 holes at both ends of MATE body, install grab irons as shown with DA 2206 eye pins

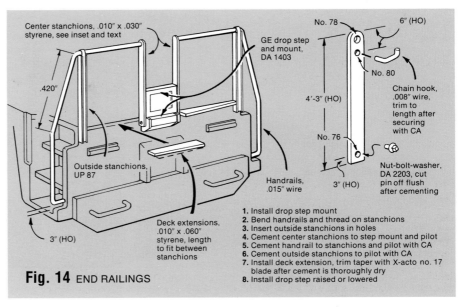

Center stanchions, .010" x .030" styrene, see inset and text

GE drop step and mount, DA 1403

No. 78

6" (HO)

.420"

No. 80

Chain hook, .008" wire, trim to length after securing with CA

4'-3" (HO)

No. 76

Outside stanchions, UP 87

3" (HO)

Handrails, .015" wire

3" (HO)

Deck extensions, .010" x .060" styrene, length to fit between stanchions

Nut-bolt-washer, DA 2203, cut pin off flush after cementing

1. Install drop step mount
2. Bend handrails and thread on stanchions
3. Insert outside stanchions in holes
4. Cement center stanchions to step mount and pilot
5. Cement hand rail to stanchions and pilot with CA
6. Cement outside stanchions to pilot with CA
7. Cement deck extension, trim taper with X-acto no. 17 blade after cement is thoroughly dry
8. Install drop step raised or lowered

Fig. 14 END RAILINGS

Kitbashing an SD45T-2 in HO scale

A. L. Schmidt

Joe Dwyer's HO scale model of Southern Pacific SD45T-2 no. 9214 was kitbashed from an Athearn SD40T-2 and a variety of Cannon & Co. parts.

Athearn's Tunnel Motor is the starting point

BY JOE DWYER

A PHOTO I shot of Southern Pacific's SD45T-2 no. 9214 piqued my interest in modeling the engine in HO scale. Later I ran across the July 1972 issue of MODEL RAILROADER (out of print), which featured photos and drawings of the SD45T-2.

The second edition of *Diesel Locomotive Rosters: U. S., Canada, Mexico* (Kalmbach Publishing Co.) lists 243 of these engines belonging to the Southern Pacific and its subsidiary, the St. Louis Southwestern Ry. (also known as the Cotton Belt). Here's how I kitbashed no. 9214 in HO scale, starting with Athearn's SD40T-2.

Kelly R. Martin

Southern Pacific 9254 shows off the Tunnel Motor radiator section that makes the SD45T-2 unique.

CHASSIS

I eased into the kitbash by starting with the chassis. After removing the motor and trucks, I needed to make only a few modifications to the frame. I started by grinding a scale 39"-long and 6"-deep section along the forward right side of the frame as shown in fig. 1. This made room for the cab assembly. Next, I cut off the coupler mounts to accommodate body-mounted couplers. I also cut off the mounting pins for the body and reassembled the chassis.

While I had the chassis separate from the body, I added detail parts to each side of the fuel tank, such as fillers, gauges, and sight glasses. See fig. 1 for placement. I also assembled the truck sideframes. Then I set the chassis aside and went to work on the body.

BODY CUTS

To begin the bodywork I started with a short-nose SD40T-2 shell. The long-nose version has the correct distance between the pilot face and the nose, but the short nose has the correct pilot. Using the long nose also requires too many modifications, so the short nose is easier to work with.

I always like to use a decorated shell so I can see lines drawn on the body. If you use an undecorated shell, you may

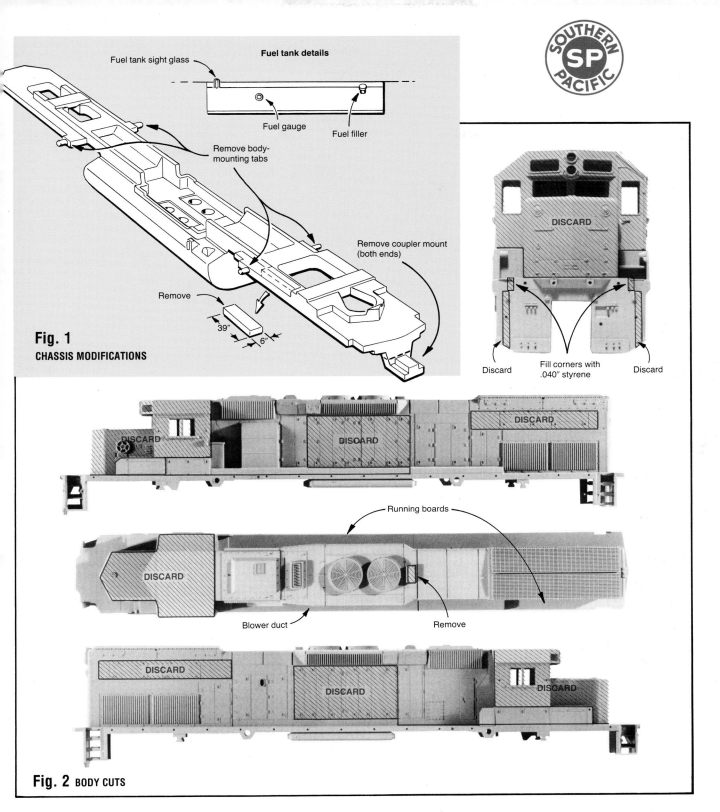

Fuel tank details

Fuel tank sight glass

Fuel gauge

Fuel filler

Remove body-mounting tabs

Remove coupler mount (both ends)

Remove

39″

6″

Fig. 1
CHASSIS MODIFICATIONS

DISCARD

Fill corners with .040″ styrene

Discard   Discard

DISCARD

DISCARD

DISCARD

DISCARD

Running boards

DISCARD

Blower duct   Remove

DISCARD   DISCARD   DISCARD

Fig. 2 BODY CUTS

want to spray it with gray primer for the same effect.

The SD45T-2 long hood is 36″ longer than the SD40T-2's; therefore, the model's long hood had to be lengthened. After removing the dynamic brake blister, I made the cuts shown in fig. 2 using a razor saw.

The third through tenth doors of the SD45T-2 are 22″ wide. The SD40T-2's

doors are 18″ wide and had to be replaced with Cannon & Co. doors. I removed the Athearn doors by cutting horizontally along the blower duct on the left and just above the bottom of the door on the right, leaving the section between the door and running board.

I threw away the doors and filed the remaining surfaces straight and square. I also removed the entire nose section at

this time to be replaced with a Cannon & Co. nose later.

Next, I cut out the radiator fan access doors on both sides. The SD45T-2 has three doors per side rather than two like the SD40T-2. Take care cutting along the top of the doors so you don't damage the rivets. I filed these surfaces smooth and square. I also trimmed off the engine room vent for

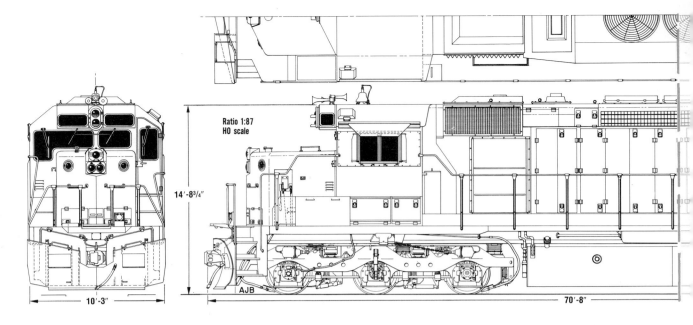

Ratio 1:87
HO scale

14'-8¾"

10'-3"

AJB

70'-8"

later replacement with a Detail Associates part.

The last cut is on the front pilot. I cut a scale 7″ section from each side flush with the second step from the bottom. Don't cut any part of the step. Figure 2 shows how I filled the top two corners with styrene, filed the corners round, and sanded them smooth.

NOSE AND CAB CONSTRUCTION

With all the hacking and slicing done, I reassembled the body, starting with the nose and working my way back to the radiator. I used the Cannon 81″ nose-conversion kit to replace the nose cut off earlier. I also used a Cannon cab.

The equipment doors under the cab on the Athearn model have to be changed, as the SD40T-2 has one door per side while the SD45T-2 has two. Complicating things further, the right side of the SD45T-2 has equal-width doors but the left side doors are unequal. Figure 3 shows how I made the

new doors using the top and bottom of a Cannon no. 1006 door.

After I built my SD45T-2, Smokey Valley came out with ready-made equipment doors (part no. 63) that can be used instead of the Cannon doors.

I removed the old equipment doors on the body and enough plastic below them so the new doors would fit flush with the adjacent panel and cab. The left side follows the same procedure as the right, except that I kept the forward part of the original door.

Since the cab is being shifted forward, an open space on the frame is exposed that needs filling. I glued in a square of .005″ styrene just forward of the right running board.

The Cannon nose needs a square section removed at the top to make room for the SP-style headlight casting. I drilled out the lower two lights of the casting with a no. 50 drill bit for later lighting.

Then I glued the hand brake in place. I added grab irons to the cab and nose

at this time since a drill wouldn't easily clear the cab number boards once they were glued in place.

BODY ASSEMBLY

Having finished the nose and cab, I assembled the rest of the body. I positioned the body on the chassis to give me a square fit of the other parts that make up the body.

The nose, cab, and forward long-hood structure are glued onto the running board first, but I test-fit everything before applying cement. Figure 4 shows the position of the nose and cab in relation to the pilot.

While all that was drying, I made the long-hood door assemblies using two pieces of .010″ styrene for the sides. I arranged the Cannon doors as shown in fig. 4 and put a border around the doors with .005″ styrene.

I filled in the blower duct gap on the left side of the engine with two pieces of .040″ styrene glued together. The running board on top of the duct is made of .005″ styrene, with the outside edge slightly indented to match the Athearn body.

After the front superstructure had dried, I added the door assemblies to the body. The interior of the door assembly must be flush with the adjacent surfaces so it won't interfere with the motor. The exterior door surface should be flush. I also added the dynamic brake. Test-fit it before gluing to ensure a level fit on top of the doors.

Working my way rearward, I built the six new radiator fan access doors as shown in fig. 4 from the backs of Cannon no. 1005 doors. I shaved off the hinges, being careful to keep the door edges intact. Next, I cut the doors to a scale length of 54″.

The access door area cut out earlier was filled with sheet styrene. I glued

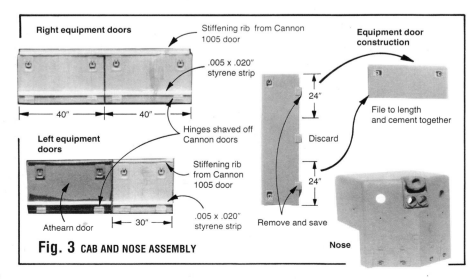

Right equipment doors

Stiffening rib from Cannon 1005 door

.005 x .020″ styrene strip

Equipment door construction

40″   40″

Left equipment doors

Hinges shaved off Cannon doors

Stiffening rib from Cannon 1005 door

24″

Discard

File to length and cement together

24″

Athearn door

30″

.005 x .020″ styrene strip

Remove and save

Fig. 3 CAB AND NOSE ASSEMBLY

Nose

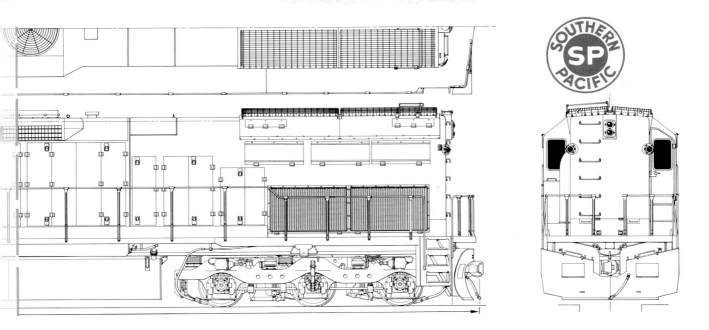

SOUTHERN SP PACIFIC

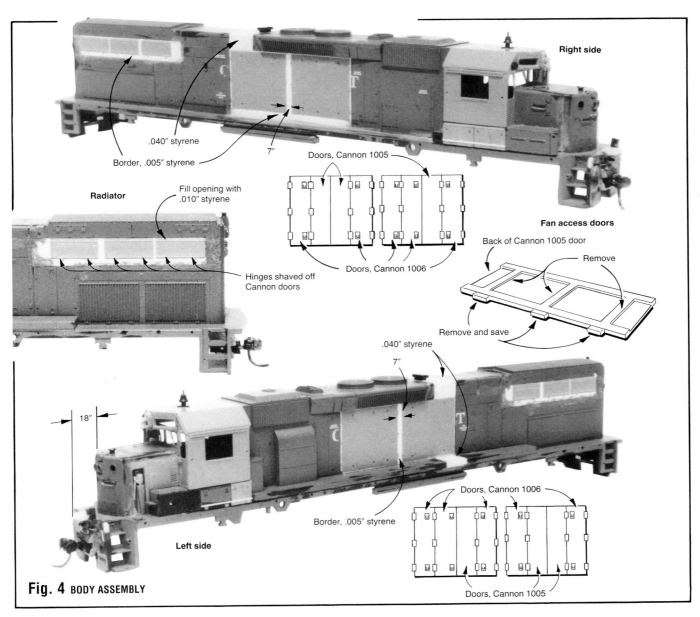

Right side

.040″ styrene

Border, .005″ styrene

7″

Doors, Cannon 1005

Radiator

Fill opening with .010″ styrene

Hinges shaved off Cannon doors

Doors, Cannon 1006

Fan access doors

Back of Cannon 1005 door

Remove

Remove and save

.040″ styrene

7″

18″

Border, .005″ styrene

Doors, Cannon 1006

Left side

Doors, Cannon 1005

Fig. 4 BODY ASSEMBLY

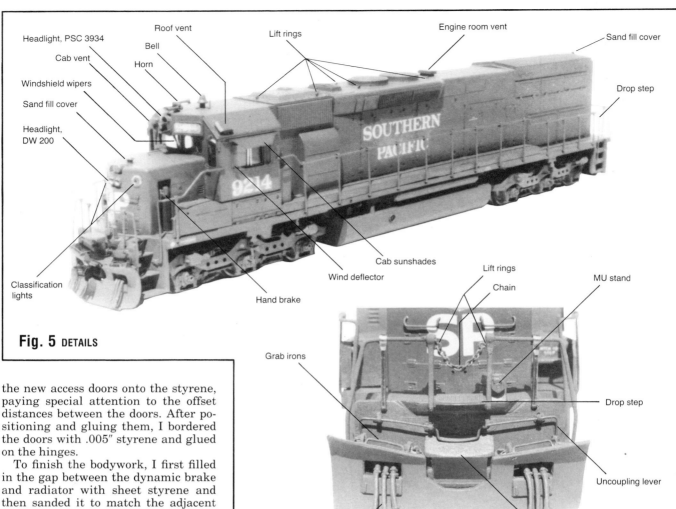

Headlight, PSC 3934
Roof vent
Lift rings
Engine room vent
Sand fill cover
Cab vent
Bell
Horn
Windshield wipers
Sand fill cover
Headlight, DW 200
Drop step
SOUTHERN PACIFIC
9214
Cab sunshades
Wind deflector
Classification lights
Hand brake
Lift rings
Chain
MU stand
Grab irons
Drop step
Uncoupling lever
MU cables
Coupler pocket

Fig. 5 DETAILS

the new access doors onto the styrene, paying special attention to the offset distances between the doors. After positioning and gluing them, I bordered the doors with .005″ styrene and glued on the hinges.

To finish the bodywork, I first filled in the gap between the dynamic brake and radiator with sheet styrene and then sanded it to match the adjacent hood contours.

DETAILING

At this stage I added the detail parts, figuring these particular ones would be easier to fasten onto the shell before painting. See fig. 5 for their locations.

Starting with the coupler pockets, I filed away the flash on the sides and glued them in place on the body with cyanoacrylate adhesive (CA). When that had dried, I tapped the pockets for 2-56 screws to hold the couplers.

Since I cut off the frame-mounting pins, I didn't need those unsightly mounting tabs on the shell. I filled them with styrene, cut them off flush, and sanded them smooth.

I trimmed off all the cast-on grab irons with a sharp hobby knife. Then I drilled holes where the ends of the original grabs were and inserted formed-wire grab irons.

Next, I filled in and sanded smooth the original handrail stanchion holes. I drilled new holes with a no. 68 bit. Use the guide in fig. 6 for the new holes.

The last step before painting was adding the stanchions and handrails. I used the original handrails, but the long ones needed extensions. I made mine with .015″ brass wire and then

soldered the extensions between the stanchions. Be patient with this process — I've found that it pays to practice on some spare wire first.

The front and rear handrails take a bit of doing too. I cut out the middle of each handrail and replaced it with chain. Then I soldered the resulting ends to the stanchions and glued metal eyebolts to the end of each short handrail. I snipped out part of each eyebolt and hung a 36″ section of HO scale chain between them.

The cab handrails need be shortened on only the horizontal part of the rail. I cut out approximately 20″ of the stock handrail's length and bent the remainder to go in the hole in the cab.

PAINTING

After washing the shell with warm soapy water and letting it air-dry, I airbrushed the body with Floquil Barrier to protect the unpainted styrene.

I like to spray on a thin coat of primer to check for flaws in sanding or

filling. I use Floquil Zinc Chromate Primer for this. If it turns out to be necessary to make corrections, I wet-sand with 600-grit paper and reapply the primer as necessary.

Once satisfied, I sprayed the entire shell, chassis (less motor and trucks), and truck sideframes with Floquil SP *Lark* Dark Grey. I left the shell to dry in direct sunlight for two days.

The nose and rear end are masked off for SP Scarlet. I used drafter's masking tape because it has a fine straight edge and less adhesive than normal tape. I painted the "wings" on the nose of my engine, but you can use Microscale decal set no. 447 if you don't want to mask the wings but you'll still have to paint the ends of the hoods.

I sprayed the nose and the end of the long hood SP Scarlet and let the paint dry for two days. Meanwhile, I painted the frames of the separate sliding windows for the Cannon cab with Aluminum.

Next, I sprayed on a coat of Glaze, thinning it with Dio-Sol, to give a

Joe Dwyer

This photo of Southern Pacific 9214 inspired the author to model the same engine. While the model is much cleaner than the prototype, all the details are faithful to the real locomotive.

smooth surface for decaling. I've found that Glaze works just as well as Crystal-Cote, and it has a drying time of only 20 minutes.

After that had dried, I applied the decals. I use Accu-set decal setting solution. Don't apply the solution on the model prior to applying the decal as the directions state. Microscale decals are very thin, and the solution will start softening the decal before you have a chance to position it.

While the solution is doing its stuff, it's a good time to make cleats for mounting the body as shown in fig. 6. Using CA, I attached a block of styrene

on the remaining coupler tab at each end of the chassis. This must be level with the coupler once it's installed. Next, I cut out a piece of .010″ brass, drilled a no. 43 hole in it, and then placed it between the screw and the top of the coupler.

I sprayed on a coat of Floquil Flat Finish, covering the chassis and truck sideframes too. After installing the windows, lenses, classification lights, and sliding windows, I reassembled the model.

The SD45T-2 was fun to build and makes an impressive addition to my HO scale SP roster. I think you'll enjoy building one too. ₲

Brass cleat, 24″ x 33″

Styrene block, .020″ x .040″

Fig. 6 MOUNTING THE BODY

Bill of materials

Athearn
4504 SD40T-2 powered undec.

Accu-paint
AP1 Stencil White
AP40 Aluminum

Builders In Scale
251 chain

Cannon & Co.
1005 doors
1006 doors
1103 81″ low nose
1501 Dash-2 cab

Detail Associates
1020 classification lights
1201 bell
1301 cab sunshades
1404 drop steps
1505 m.u. stand
1902 cab vent
1903 roof vent
1904 engine room vent
2202 grab irons
2204 uncoupling lever
2206 lift rings
2304 wind deflector
3001 sand fill covers
3101 fuel gauge

Details West
132 hand brake
140 snow plow
166 fuel filler
175 horn
200 headlight

Floquil paint
110132 SP *Lark* Dark Grey
110136 SP Scarlet
110601 Zinc Chromate Primer

Kadee
5 couplers

Microscale
87-11 SP decal set

Precision Scale Co.
3934 headlight
3967 windshield wipers

Warren's Custom Services
8000 coupler pocket
8007 m.u. cables
8012 fuel tank sight glass

Miscellaneous
.005″ styrene
.010″ styrene
.010″ sheet brass
.015″-diameter wire
.040″ styrene

Action Red GP38

Modeling a CP Rail Geep in HO scale

BY GERRY GILLILAND
MODEL PHOTOS BY THE AUTHOR

CP RAIL GP38s have many distinctive features that aren't hard to duplicate and give a model special appeal. As for any modeling project, research is the

key to realism. My sources of information included *Rail Canada Vol. 3*, the *Second Diesel Spotter's Guide* (Kalmbach Publishing Co.), and the *MODEL RAILROADER Cyclopedia: Vol. 2, Diesel Locomotives* (Kalmbach). I modeled engine 3018 following a photo in the *MODEL RAILROADER Cyclopedia* (reproduced here). It's one of a group of 21, nos. 3000-3020, that were built in 1970 and 1971 by General Motors Diesel Ltd. in London, Ontario.

An Athearn GP38-2 with dynamic brakes was the starting point for this

project. The Athearn cab has the Dash 2-style rear overhang, so I replaced it with a Cannon thin-wall "35 line" cab following the manufacturer's instructions. The cab and nose details are shown in fig. 1. I made my own snow shields for the air intakes from .020″ styrene, only to learn afterwards that Details West makes them — the part number is in the bill of materials.

Athearn has, of course, modeled the Dash 2-style access doors and battery-box covers below and in front of the cab. I chose to ignore these, but I did

James A. Brown

CP Rail's GP38s were the first of this model in Canada. At Toronto in 1970, brand-new 3000 and 3001 wear the original full-height multi-marks and associated end striping.

When MR's Jim Hediger photographed CP Rail 3018 at Winnepeg, Manitoba, in 1977, the GP38
had been repainted with the smaller version of the corporate "multi-mark" at the rear end.

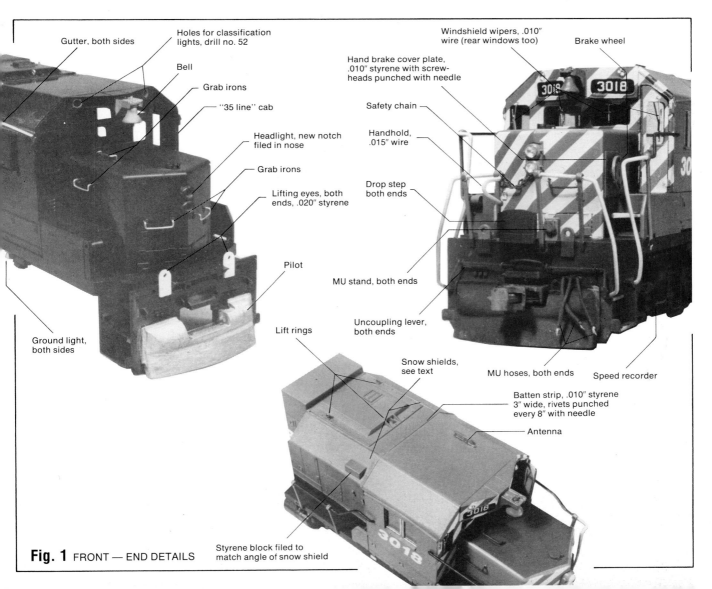

Gutter, both sides

Holes for classification
lights, drill no. 52

Bell

Grab irons

"35 line" cab

Headlight, new notch
filed in nose

Grab irons

Lifting eyes, both
ends, .020" styrene

Pilot

Ground light,
both sides

Lift rings

Snow shields,
see text

Windshield wipers, .010"
wire (rear windows too)

Brake wheel

Hand brake cover plate,
.010" styrene with screw-
heads punched with needle

Safety chain

Handhold,
.015" wire

Drop step
both ends

MU stand, both ends

Uncoupling lever,
both ends

MU hoses, both ends

Speed recorder

Batten strip, .010" styrene
3" wide, rivets punched
every 8" with needle

Antenna

Styrene block filed to
match angle of snow shield

Fig. 1 FRONT — END DETAILS

53

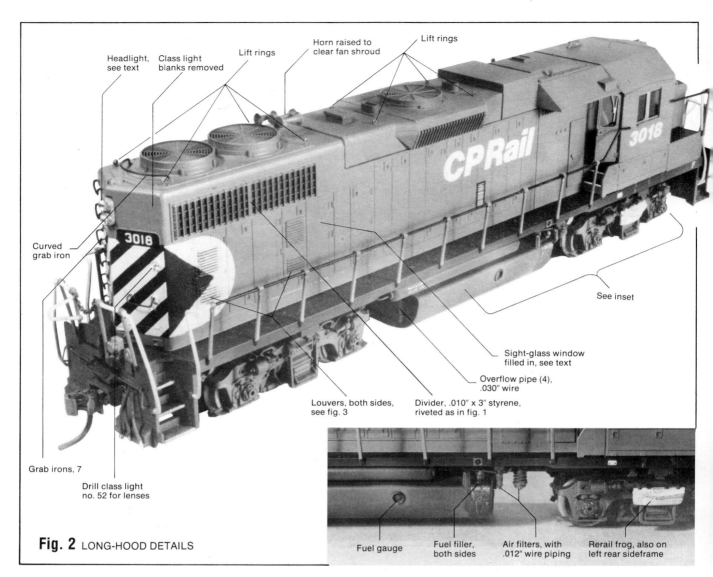

Headlight, see text

Class light blanks removed

Lift rings

Horn raised to clear fan shroud

Lift rings

Curved grab iron

3018

CP Rail

3018

See inset

Sight-glass window filled in, see text

Overflow pipe (4), .030" wire

Louvers, both sides, see fig. 3

Divider, .010" x 3" styrene, riveted as in fig. 1

Grab irons, 7

Drill class light no. 52 for lenses

Fig. 2 LONG-HOOD DETAILS

Fuel gauge

Fuel filler, both sides

Air filters, with .012" wire piping

Rerail frog, also on left rear sideframe

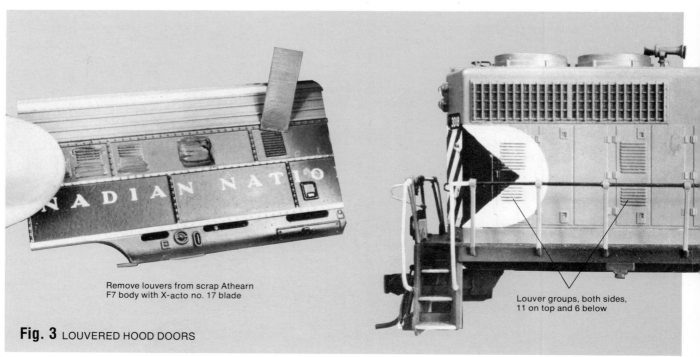

Remove louvers from scrap Athearn F7 body with X-acto no. 17 blade

Louver groups, both sides, 11 on top and 6 below

Fig. 3 LOUVERED HOOD DOORS

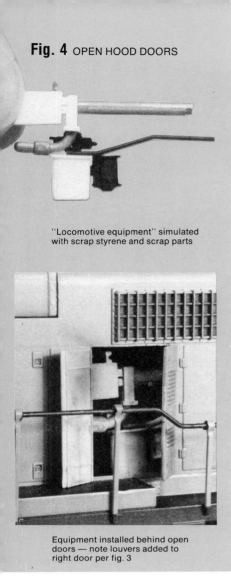

Fig. 4 OPEN HOOD DOORS

"Locomotive equipment" simulated with scrap styrene and scrap parts

Equipment installed behind open doors — note louvers added to right door per fig. 3

get rid of the more obvious Dash 2 sight-glass window on the right side of the hood. I backed the opening with .010" styrene, filled the window with auto spot putty, then sanded it smooth. This and other long-hood details are shown in fig. 2.

To replace the horizontal headlight on the rear end, I first filled the holes with round sprues, then filed the light away to match the vee of the end. Then I filed a notch for the new headlight as on the nose.

The louvered doors at the rear are special features of the CPR GP38s. Figure 3 shows how I took louvers from a scrap body with a chisel blade. After sanding them as thin as I could without having them fall apart, I attached them with sparing amounts of Testor's liquid cement. Use too much cement, and the louvers end up as blobs of plastic.

The open doors on the left side of the hood, fig. 4, are an eye-catching special effect. I cut out the two doors, then filed the inside edges of the body opening for a thin, crisp look. Using a photograph

as a guide, and some scrap pieces of plastic, I made a reasonable facsimile of what was behind those doors. This assembly has to be kept thin so it won't interfere with the operation of the locomotive.

While I added parts to the modified GP truck sideframes that came with the model for a more realistic look, they still aren't really correct. You'd do better to substitute Athearn's standard GP truck sideframes, the so-called "Blomberg B" type, no. 42009.

ACTION RED

The body was washed in warm soapy water and allowed to air-dry, then I primed it with a spray of Floquil no. 110084 Foundation. After a week or so, I airbrushed it with SMP Industries Accu-paint no. 11 CP Rail Action Red.

When the Action Red had dried, I masked the nose, cab, hood, and the side of the raised walkway duct to keep them red. Everything from the walkways down is black, and I airbrushed these parts with Accu-paint no. 2 Stencil Black. Then I masked around the top of the nose and sprayed it Floquil no. 110013 Grimy Black to represent nonskid black. I also painted the underframe and truck sideframes with Grimy Black. The equipment behind the open hood doors is painted a light gray, along with the insides of the hood and cab doors.

SMP's Accu-cals Multipak No. 5824H decal set supplied the "multi-marks," striping, numbers, and lettering. Note that these GP38s were delivered with large CP multi-marks extending from the walkway to the top of the hood. By 1975 they were being repainted with the smaller multi-marks that I used.

After the decals were applied, I gave the model a coat of Floquil no. 110015 Flat Finish. To give the grills and fans some depth, I first brush-painted them with Polly S Grimy Black. After letting this dry for several minutes, I used a damp cloth to wipe off the grills, leaving Grimy Black in the recesses. I used this technique on the door louvers also.

Finishing up involved installing the cab glazing, painting the windshield wipers silver and installing them, and installing and hand-painting the handrails and stanchions. Notice that the stanchions are black below the line of the side and end sills. The headlight and classification light lenses were added, along with the m.u. hoses and the m.u. stands, which I painted separately. I used Walthers Goo to mount the cab and hood doors in open positions, something that adds a lot to the model.

I used Floquil no. 110073 Rust to paint the couplers, and diluted it with Dio-Sol to spot-wash the trucks and pilots. The engine roof, trucks, and pilots were given a light misting of Floquil

Bill of materials

Athearn
4600 GP38-2, undecorated with dynamic brake

Campbell Scale Models
256 chain

Cannon & Co.
1003 hood door
1004 hood door
1502 35 line cab

Detail Associates
1004 headlights
1404 drop steps
1505 m.u. stands
1508 m.u. hoses
1803 antenna
2202 grab irons
2206 wire eyebolts (lift rings)
2211 uncoupling levers
2807 speed recorder drive
3101 fuel gauge
6503 curved grab iron

Details West
139 air filter set
166 fuel fillers
172 step lights (ground lights)
179 brake wheel
194 snow shields

Kadee
5 couplers

Juneco*
29 pilot
33 rerailing frogs

Miniatures by Eric**
2 bell
21 horn

MV Products
22 classification light lenses
25 headlight lenses

*Juneco Scale Models
  Inter-Hobbies Dist.
  RR 1
  Martintown, Ontario
  Canada K0C 1S0

**Miniatures by Eric
  32 Clarendon Rd. N. W.
  Calgary, Alberta
  Canada T2L 0P1

Grimy Black. I wanted to represent an engine that has not been in service too long since repainting.

I highlighted the sideframes with Floquil no. 110006 Dust to bring out the details. As a final weathering step, I mixed Floquil no. 110010 Engine Black with no. 110003 Hi-Gloss and streaked it down the sides of the fuel tank at the fillers. The Hi-Gloss gives the wet look of fresh-spilled fuel.

And that completed my CP Rail Action Red GP38. Good luck with your own model. ₥

New splash of color for CSX locomotives

Painting (and building) an HO scale B36-7

When one of today's "Super Seven" rail systems unveils a new locomotive paint scheme and launches a major repainting program, that's big news. CSX Transportation treated it that way, too, announcing the new livery with press releases including a photo color chips, a paint diagram, and even photos of the various older schemes that are being replaced.

CSX Transportation came into being with the merger of the Chessie and Seaboard Systems in 1986. Its first blue-and-gray locomotive scheme appeared that year, but CSX considers that one and its subsequent variations as experiments. Most notorious of these was the almost-solid-gray "stealth" scheme that may have been cost-effective and practical, but didn't seem to be promoting a positive image for the railroad.

Then on March 26, 1990, B36-7 no. 5895 rolled out of the paint shop in Waycross, Ga., in what CSX describes as "the company's final choice" for a locomotive paint design. The blue and gray remain, but with bold yellow accents that both brighten the appearance and improve visibility.

CSX photo by John B. Corns

The first unit in the new CSX paint scheme was B36-7 no. 5895, but over 450 locomotives will be in these colors by year's end. Thank the company photographer for the unusual view.

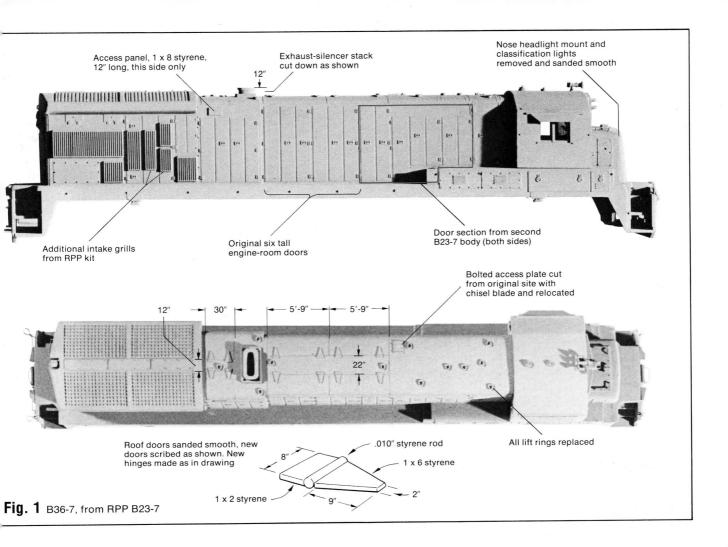

Access panel, 1 x 8 styrene, 12" long, this side only

Exhaust-silencer stack cut down as shown

12"

Nose headlight mount and classification lights removed and sanded smooth

Additional intake grills from RPP kit

Original six tall engine-room doors

Door section from second B23-7 body (both sides)

Bolted access plate cut from original site with chisel blade and relocated

12"   30"   5'-9"   5'-9"

22"

Roof doors sanded smooth, new doors scribed as shown. New hinges made as in drawing

All lift rings replaced

8"   .010" styrene rod

1 x 6 styrene

1 x 2 styrene   9"   2"

Fig. 1 B36-7, from RPP B23-7

The blue band wrapping over the cab at an angle adds impact, and the corporate logo stands out in 55"-high letters on the side of the hood. For the operating department, the bright yellow cab numerals make the unit's number easy to read, and for diesel spotters there's a model-designation stencil just below.

CSX intended to have the new image take hold quickly, and set the goal of having 400 units repainted by the end of 1990. In addition, new locomotives purchased in 1990, including 50 General Electric Dash 8-40Cs, also arrived in the new paint. Even the system's "executive" F units, FP7 118 and F7 booster 119, have been repainted.

Jay Brown

On an EMD locomotive, the new colors look as shown on GP40-2 no. 6400. There's more yellow on the nose, but the stripe is thinner on EMD's shallower side sill. The top of the blue band is 24" above the walkway, and the blue wraps over the left-side walkway duct.

Alan Brandenburger

B36-7 Model

I set out to make an HO model of the first unit in the new paint. Decals were no problem, because Microscale had been helping in the development of the new scheme and had its 1990 CSX set ready by the time the railroad's news release was in the mail.

Locomotive 5895 was another story. This B36-7 is one of 120, nos. 5806–5925, built for fast intermodal service on the Seaboard System in 1985. While models of modern GEs are easier to come by now than they were even a few years ago, the B36-7 is one that's still not available. Rail Power Products does have a B23-7 body kit to fit Athearn's U-boat chassis, and photos and drawings showed that the "23" could be converted into a reasonable facsimile of its 3,600-hp big brother.

The main thing, it seems to me, is to have the correct number of tall engine-room doors, eight per side, and the matching power-assembly doors on the roof. Figure 1 shows how I went about it, using doors taken from a second B23-7 body. My model isn't exactly right as far as the hinge and latch arrangement on the engine-room doors, but it looks right under all but the closest scrutiny.

The kits and parts for this project are listed in the bill of materials. The only parts of the Athearn kit that I used were the power chassis and handrail stanchions, and another option would be to use a Proto Power West U-boat chassis and buy the stanchions separately—from Walthers, not Athearn.

I cut the coupler mounts off the underframe and body-mounted the Kadee couplers, using the longer no. 26 in front to clear the plow. To mount the body, I cemented blocks of styrene inside the ends of the hood, then drilled through the underframe and tapped the blocks for one 1-72 flathead machine screw at each end. The body needed some styrene shims to level it on the chassis, a minor adjustment. The walkway deck should be about 5'-8" above the rail.

Detailing

Now it's all a matter of details and paint, and the details are shown in fig. 2. The real 5895 has a five-chime air horn in a low-profile mount, and the Detail Associates three-chime horn I used seemed the closest compromise. Sure enough, as soon as my model was painted Bowser announced a new CalScale air horn that's just right, and it's a sturdy brass casting, too.

I bent my own handrails following RPP's instructions and soldered them

---

Bill of materials

Rail Power Products
B23-7 body shell, 2

Athearn
3400 U28B (or any four-axle GE)

Cal-Scale
427 air horn (see text)

Campbell Scale Models
256 black chain

Detail Associates
1202 bell
1403 drop steps
1503 m.u. stands
1507 m.u. receptacles
1508 m.u. hoses
1709 class light lenses (headlight)
1802 whip antenna bases
2202 drop grab irons
2206 wire eyebolts
2304 wind screens
2502 .010" brass wire
2504 .012" brass wire
2505 .015" brass wire
2506 .019" brass wire
6210 straight grab irons
101301 brass sunshades

Details West
117 headlight (backup light)
139 air filter set
149 fuel fillers

179 brake wheel
203 sand filler hatches
207 plow

Evergreen Scale Models styrene
224 ⅛" tube
8102 HO 1 x 2
8106 HO 1 x 6
8108 HO 1 x 8
8206 HO 2 x 6
9015 .015" sheet

Kadee
5 coupler
26 coupler

MV Products
19 lenses (for backup light)

Plastruct styrene
1310 .010" rod
1330 .030" rod

Precision Scale Co.
3933 headlight with visors
3967 brass windshield wipers,
  2 pkgs.

Smokey Valley RR & Machine Co.
112 FB-2 sideframes

Utah Pacific
62 lift rings, 2 pkgs.

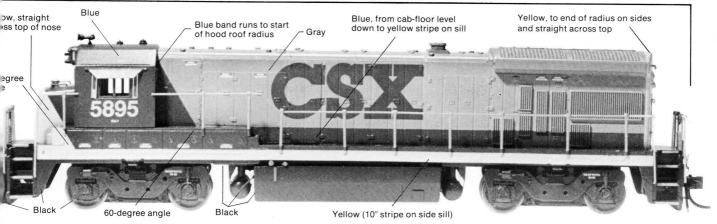

ow, straight
ss top of nose   Blue

    Blue band runs to start
    of hood roof radius   Gray

Blue, from cab-floor level
down to yellow stripe on sill

Yellow, to end of radius on sides
and straight across top

egree
e

5895

Black   60-degree angle   Black   Yellow (10″ stripe on side sill)

AINT DETAILS	All walkway surfaces blue
	All step edges yellow
	Grab irons match background color,
	   except for yellow grabs on plow
	Handles and shafts of uncoupling
	   levers yellow
		Handrails gray, except yellow from
		   step well to first stanchion
		Stanchions gray, except painted to
		   match background below walkways
		Fuel fillers, gauges, and cutoff buttons red
			LETTERING	55″ blue logo on side of hood
				20″ blue logo on ends
				16″ yellow numerals on cab
				2″ yellow model designation below
				   numerals on cab ("B36-7")
				5″ black "F" at front of side sill

blue onto some blank decal scraps. Then it was on to the black, which includes the pilots, step wells, step skirts, jacking pads, plow, underframe, and truck sideframes. That lower section of the side sill at the left front is also black. The bottom edge of the yellow stripe extends in a straight line here, and the small area left over is painted black. Meanwhile, back at the handrails, I used Hobsco Magic Masker to cover the yellow ends up to the first stanchions, and then gave the railings and stanchions yet another coat of gray. The first coat of gray was a base for the yellow, and this one is the final color — almost.

Lettering

After giving the body, cab, and sideframes a clear gloss finish of Floquil Crystal-Cote, I applied the Microscale decals according to the maker's instructions. The only fault in the decals is that the letters in the logos run together, but should have thin but distinct spaces in between. I cut the letters apart and applied them individually, which also helps the decals settle onto the surface detail.

The decal sheet includes a lot of small lettering that adds interest. A yellow "WATCH YOUR STEP" warning goes on each cab door, and there's white gear-ratio lettering for the sideframes — it's 83-20 for the B36-7, but others are included.

The small blue lettering on the right side goes as follows: fifth door back from cab, "ENGINE START SWITCH INSIDE"; first door on wide section of hood, "FIRE EXTINGUISHER INSIDE"; and third door back on wide section, "ENGINE WATER FILL INSIDE." Photographs don't show any similar lettering on the left side of 5895, but there are plenty of those red-and-white "DANGER HIGH VOLTAGE" signs on both sides. I took these from the Microscale Rio Grande Ski Train set because they come in one piece, a big help on a unit that has 15 of the darned things!

Remember that blank decal paper I painted yellow? That provided the yellow step edging. Microscale's white number boards don't match the RPP moldings, so I cut pieces of white decal stripe to fit. After applying the numbers, I used a black Sharpie indelible marker to outline the raised gaskets.

Winding up

Now I assembled the hood and cab added the handrails and the rest of the details, and reassembled the chassis, doing the necessary detail and touchup painting as I went. Lengths of solder drape nicely as the m.u. jumper cables and look convincing in Floquil Oxide Red. The cover of the live m.u.

receptacle, on the right as you face the pilot, is red. The cover on the dummy receptacle to the right is green. Both covers are still red in Art Schmidt's model photo, but then I finally noticed my mistake and corrected it.

CSX paints the bottom ends of its gray stanchions to match the background color below the walkways. That was easy to do with a brush everywhere except along the side sills, where there should be a neat blue stripe between the gray and the yellow. I brushed the lower ends of those stanchions yellow, then added 4″ x 8″ pieces of my blue-painted decal paper.

Almost finished now, I gave the body and chassis a sealing spray of Crystal-Cote for a newly painted look. While that dried, I painted the wind screens silver and used Microscale Kristal-Kleer to glaze them. Their top and bottom tabs are bent over and inserted directly into holes in the cab; the tiny etchings are too delicate to "operate."

I glazed the cab windows with clear plastic, put MV lenses in the backup light, and inserted Detail Associates clear-plastic lenses in the headlight. These work nicely with a bulb in a short length of brass tube inside the cab. With the locomotive together at last, I could step back and take a look. Nice job, CSX. — *Andy Sperandeo*

Chris Becker

Indiana Harbor Belt EMD switcher

An HO scale SW1500 in the dark green and orange scheme

BY DAVID JISKRA

The Indiana Harbor Belt uses a fleet of Electro-Motive Division switchers to handle its transfer and switching runs around Chicago. In the mid-1980s, the railroad reversed the colors of its previous paint scheme, making the locomotive color dark green (almost black) with orange lettering and striping.

I wanted to paint an HO scale locomotive in this new scheme. Since the IHB operates more SW1500s (23) than any other locomotive type, I decided to model one of those units.

Modeling

I started with an undecorated Athearn SW1500. The stock model comes with Flexicoil truck sideframes, which must be replaced with Athearn no. 41021 AAR type A sideframes. I also discarded the plastic bell that comes with the engine. All of the IHB SW1500s that I've seen have a plow on the front (hood) end,

and some units have plows on both ends.

As the photos show, the small side windows, the two center front windows, and the lower left-side and lower door windows on the cab rear need to be plugged. I traced outlines of the window openings onto scraps of .040" styrene, cut and filed these to a snug fit, then used liquid plastic cement to glue them in place.

I used small amounts of Squadron Green body putty to fill gaps. I added the horn and antenna, added a sunshade over the fireman's-side window, and set the cab aside.

I used an X-acto no. 17 chisel blade to remove the cast-on uncoupling lever and m.u. stubs from the pilots. I filed smooth the lower portion of the front pilot and drilled holes for mounting the plow. Then I drilled holes for the m.u. hoses and uncoupling-lever brackets and installed the uncoupling levers. Using a no. 80 bit,

I drilled holes for all of the wire grab irons, except for the top rung on the side hood.

Handrails

The most noticeable difference between the Athearn model and the IHB prototype is the handrails. The model uses full-length outside handrails, but the Harbor units have handrails mounted on the hood sides.

I used putty to fill in the stanchion holes along the side sills, except for the front holes on both sides and the first hole forward of the cab on the fireman's side. I rebent the forward portion of both stock handrails as shown in fig. 1 by bending the wire 90 degrees downward. Where this passed over the sill, I drilled a new hole with a no. 70 bit. Then I made a final 90-degree bend toward the sill, cut the rail, and checked the fit.

The fireman's side has an additional

Tom Golden

The Indiana Harbor Belt numbers its SW1500s 9200-9222. Here no. 9219 and slug unit 478 switch a cut of cars at Riverdale, Ill., in August 1984.

handrail in front of the cab door. Again I used the end of the stock Athearn handrail. I straightened the bend where the rail turned to run horizontally along the hood. With the cab in position, I set this handrail in place and made a downward bend to match the hole in the side sill. As with the front handrails, I made a final 90-degree bend toward the sill, cut the rail, and checked the fit.

I used .022" wire to make the new hood-mounted handrails. Each piece is 3¾" long with a bend at each end to enter holes drilled in the hood. For the supports I used Detail Associates eyebolts, three on each side, as shown in fig. 2. I drilled no. 80 holes above the gaps between the hood doors, threaded the eyebolts onto the handrail, slid everything into place, and secured it with cyanoacrylate adhesive (CA) from inside the shell.

I added the top grab irons, glued the new bell in place, and attached the m.u. stands. The Detail Associates m.u. stand has two receptacles, but the IHB units have just one, so use the bottom position only. After the glue had dried, I washed the hood and cab in warm, soapy water, thoroughly rinsed them, and allowed them to air-dry.

Paint and decals

I followed the Virnex recommendation for mixing the dark green color with Floquil paints, using 1 part Engine Black and 2 parts Brunswick Green. Unless you look at the model under very bright lighting, it's tough to tell the difference between the mixed color and straight Engine Black. Of course, it's the same for the prototype locomotives. If you think the color looks too dark, you can add more Brunswick Green to the mix.

I sprayed the entire shell and the end handrails with the mix. After the shell had dried, I masked everything except the front number board and the area between the number board and grill on top. These areas were sprayed with Reefer Orange. When the paint had dried, I applied a coat of Crystal-Cote to provide a smooth surface for decals. I also sprayed the all-weather cab window with Floquil Platinum Mist.

I started the decaling with the stripe around the cab, cutting two pieces to length and applying them and the unit numbers. The American flag under the engineer's window came from a Microscale Santa Fe set. These are only used on some IHB switchers, so check prototype photos if you're modeling another unit. I used Solvaset on these decals and let them dry.

The next step was to install the cab on the shell and lightly pencil the location of the stripe onto the hood. Refer to the prototype photo and line up the "HARBOR" as closely as possible. Then, add the stripes and remaining lettering.

It took a lot of piecing and a fair amount of Solvaset to get the decals

Bill of materials

Athearn
    3900 SW1500, undecorated
    41021 truck sideframes

Detail Associates
    1301 sunshade
    1502 m.u. stands
    1508 m.u. hoses
    1803 antenna
    2202 grab irons
    2206 eyebolts
    2211 uncoupling levers
    2301 all-weather cab window
    2507 .022" wire
    102213 uncoupling-lever brackets

Details West
    125 bell
    150 plow

Floquil paint
    110004 Crystal-Cote
    110010 Engine Black
    110011 Reefer White
    110015 Flat Finish
    110030 Reefer Orange
    110034 Brunswick Green
    110144 Platinum Mist

Kadee
    5 coupler
    26 coupler (hood end)

Microscale decals
    87093 condensed Gothic alphabet
    and numbers
    87619 Santa Fe locomotives (for flag)

MV Products
    25 lenses

Virnex decal
    6005 IHB locomotives, black scheme

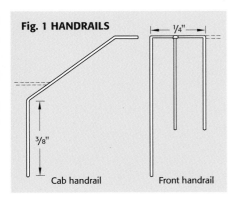

Fig. 1 HANDRAILS

¼"

⅜"

Cab handrail   Front handrail

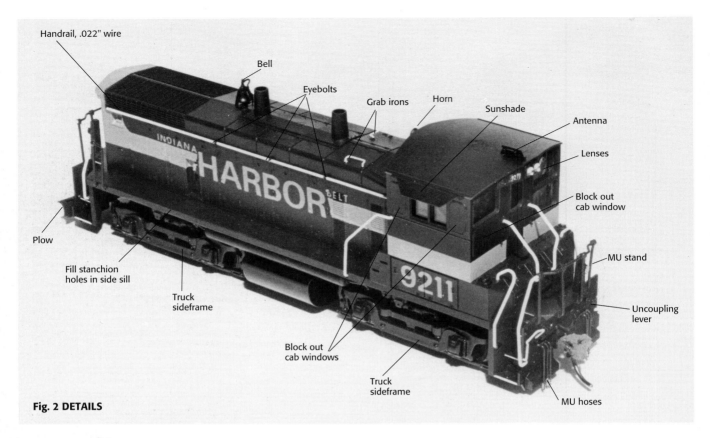

Handrail, .022" wire

Bell

Eyebolts

Grab irons

Horn

Sunshade

Antenna

Lenses

Block out cab window

Plow

Fill stanchion holes in side sill

Truck sideframe

MU stand

Uncoupling lever

Block out cab windows

Truck sideframe

MU hoses

Fig. 2 DETAILS

around the radiator. In the recessed areas, I did what I could with Solvaset, then used Reefer Orange to touch things up. I also brushed Reefer Orange on the m.u. receptacle covers.

I finished the decaling with the white decal step edges left from a previous project and the number boards, which are from a Microscale condensed

Gothic set. I poked any bubbles under the decals with a sharp hobby knife and applied more Solvaset until the decals settled into place.

I sealed the decals by spraying the model with a coat of Floquil Flat Finish. I added the cab windows, glued the all-weather window in place, and installed the lenses. Then I added the handrails

and side grab irons and brush-painted Reefer White on the appropriate handrails and grab irons. I also brush-painted the wheel sides and the metal inner truck sideframes with Engine Black.

Finally, I added the Kadee couplers to the underframe, snapped on the shell, added the plow, and my model of IHB no. 9211 was complete.

A Detroit, Toledo & Ironton GP40-2 in HO scale

Chris Becker

The DT&I kept its fast freights moving with these distinctive orange diesels

BY JIM HEDIGER

A fleet of bright orange GP40 and GP40-2 road switchers was the primary mainline motive power on the Detroit, Toledo & Ironton RR for nearly 15 years. These 3,000-hp Electro-Motive Division locomotives handled the DT&I's hot manifest freights and *Rail Blazer* piggyback trains between Detroit and Cincinnati. Since my free-lanced HO scale Ohio Southern is controlled by the DT&I, I decided the OS had to have some of these locomotives.

Prototype scheme

Bright orange has been the DT&I's standard diesel locomotive color since the early 1950s. This distinctive color was introduced after the railroad's first diesel switchers went to work in areas

that included street running. Railroad veterans recall that these black units were involved in so many accidents that the exasperated president demanded a color "everyone will notice."

Both switchers were repainted and all subsequent new locomotives were delivered in orange except for bicentennial GP38-2 no. 1776 (later renumbered 228). The orange units began to disappear shortly after the DT&I was merged into the Grand Trunk Western in December 1983, and the last orange engine was repainted in 1990.

The first locomotives to carry the 60" initials on the hood were the last order of GP9s (990-992, built in 1957). This was standard for all road switchers until 1979, when the DT&I introduced the star

herald as shown in the prototype photo of GP40 no. 407.

The DT&I's second-generation locomotives came lettered with the compass herald and "We have the connections" slogan through 1970. This slogan was dropped after the Penn Central merger eliminated many of the DT&I's connections, so new and repainted equipment between 1971 and 1979 carried the compass herald without the slogan.

As the roster shows, the DT&I bought its high-horsepower GP40s and Dash 2s in four groups. I decided to model a GP40-2 from the 1973 order. Fortunately, Athearn's GP40-2 proved to be the perfect starting point. All it needed was a few extra details and the standard DT&I paint scheme.

DT&I second-generation road switchers

Model	Nos.	Built	Slogan
GP38	207-214	1970	Yes
GP38AC	215-220	1971	No
GP38-2	221-228	1975	No
SD38	250-252	1969	Yes
SD38	253-254	1971	No
GP35	350-357	1964	Yes
GP40	400-405	1968	Yes
GP40-2	406-413	1972	No
GP40-2	414-421	1973	No
GP40-2	422-425	1979	Star herald

Jim Hediger

DT&I GP40-2 no. 418 wears the standard road-switcher scheme in 1980.

Jim Hediger

The DT&I began painting units with the star herald in 1979. One of the GP40s delivered in 1968, no. 407, received wreck repairs and was repainted in this scheme by 1983.

Chassis and shell

Two major chassis changes are necessary to get the DT&I appearance. The prototype's smaller fuel tank is best simulated by using an Athearn GP38-2 chassis. This frame is sold separately so you can move the GP40-2 trucks and motor onto it, or you can start with a GP38-2 mechanism and just add a GP40-2 shell.

The DT&I used the earlier style of GP truck. Pry off the "type M" sideframes on the model and substitute Athearn "Blomberg B" sideframes.

The nose bell, shown in fig. 1, is the most prominent feature on the shell. File a flat area into the front of the low hood and cement the plastic part in place.

Add the other details shown in figs. 1 and 2 by drilling mounting holes and securing the parts with drops of cyanoacrylate adhesive (CA).

I body-mounted Kadee no. 5 couplers in their own draft-gear boxes, using laminated styrene pads cemented behind the pilots. Mount the draft-gear boxes with 2-56 screws and use a hacksaw to cut the metal coupler-mounting brackets from each end of the frame to clear the new coupler mounts.

Painting

Airbrush the body with several light coats of Floquil SP Lettering Gray and let it dry thoroughly. Then spray the shell and battery box sides with Floquil *Daylight* Red and allow it to dry. This color is a little darker than the actual DT&I paint, but it looks correct under the incandescent lighting in my layout room.

Next, use masking tape to cover the hoods, cab, and pilots, and spray the walkways and side sills with Floquil Engine Black. Once the paint sets, remove the tape and remask the model to spray the black anti-glare panel on top of the nose.

The last step is to brush-paint the raised walkways along both sides of the short hood. I also used the brush to touch up the inside corners around the cab and steps.

Decals

I lettered my model using a Herald King set, but Des Plaines Hobbies recently released a very accurate set for these locomotives. It's listed in the bill of materials.

Trim the decals close to the image and apply the big side letters individually. Align the top of each letter with the start of the roof radius, spacing the letters evenly across the tall doors as shown in the photos.

Place the compass herald (a decal on the prototype too!) so its horizontal points are just above the access door and slightly forward, to keep the bottom vertical point out of the latch.

Apply the decals, let them sit for about 10 minutes, then add Walthers Solvaset diluted 1:1 with water using a small brush. After the decals dry, use a fresh X-acto no. 11 blade to carefully slit the decal film along the door edges. A second application of diluted Solvaset will usually draw the decals down into the details, but sometimes an additional application or two is needed to make the decal look painted on.

After the decals dry overnight, use a small brush to touch up the hinge and latch areas with black paint.

Finishing touches

The wire handrails are next. Carefully align all the stanchions and add drops of CA to keep them square. Brush-paint the

Fig. 1 DETAILS

Beacon

Horn

Lift rings

Bell

Grab iron

MU hoses

Truck sideframes

Bill of materials

Athearn
4701 GP40-2 powered kit
42009 truck sideframes
46029 GP38-2 frame

Des Plaines Hobbies
(1468 Lee St., Des Plaines, IL 60018,
708-297-2118)
DT&I-1 locomotive decals

Detail Associates
1204 bell
1508 m.u. hoses
2202 grab irons
2205 uncoupling lever
2206 lift rings
2504 .012" brass wire

Details West
106 beacon
186 horn

Floquil
110006 Dust
110010 Engine Black
110013 Grimy Black
110017 Weathered Black
110130 SP Lettering Gray
110135 SP *Daylight* Red

Herald King decals
L-110 DT&I locomotive

Kadee
5 couplers

MV products
25 headlight jewels

railings black, using a piece of cardboard to protect the hood and cab from any splatters.

A light spray coat of Floquil Flat Finish sealed the surface and provided a nice even finish.

Because of their glossy Imron paint, the prototype locomotives didn't weather heavily. I added some light weathering to the model, airbrushing several light dustings of thinned Floquil Dust, Mud, and Weathered Black along the running gear and steps to re-create the grime that the prototype diesels pick up. I also used an L-shaped card mask to cover the body while spraying a little shading into the intake screens along the upper sides. The last step was to dust the roof

with Floquil Grimy Black to simulate exhaust soot and "crud."

None of the detail changes I made are difficult, but together they turn a stock kit into a locomotive that exhibits the family appearance of my favorite prototype. The real railroad may be gone, but my model of no. 418 is now hard at work helping re-create a portion of the DT&I in my basement.

Curved grab iron, .012" wire

Grab irons

Uncoupling lever

MU hoses

Fig. 2 REAR

Hiawatha-scheme SD40-2 in HO scale

The Milwaukee Road's final paint scheme brought back the famous running Indian logo

BY KEITH FINK

The Milwaukee Road's final paint scheme retained the railroad's traditional black and orange, but incorporated a modified "lightning stripe" just behind the cab.

However, the most distinctive part of this scheme was the *Hiawatha* nose emblem, a symbol that brought the pride of the railroad's 1937 *Hiawatha* streamliners to the 1980s.

The scheme was developed in 1983 by Milwaukee Road employees Art Danz and Ed Abbott. The first locomotive to wear it, SD40-2 no. 201, emerged on Nov. 9, 1983. By the time the Soo Line purchased the Milwaukee Road on Jan. 1, 1986, 37 units had received this scheme, including 31 SD40-2s. Here's how I modeled one of them, no. 195.

Underframe

Clamp the frame in a vise and use a hacksaw to remove the front part of the fuel tank and other areas as fig. 1 shows. Remove only the shaded areas – don't trim any material above the tank itself or the frame will be weakened.

Disassemble the trucks and check the gears for burrs. I replaced the Athearn wheelsets with NorthWest Short Line nickel-plated 40" wheels.

Add the brake cylinders and shock absorbers to the sideframes. Drill no. 76 holes in the ends of each cylinder and form air lines using .020" brass wire. You can see this in the color photo.

Paint the inner metal side plates on the trucks black, and paint the wheel faces with Accu-Flex Grimy Black.

Install the fuel gauge (engineer's side only) and fuel fillers. Add the fuel sight glasses and the spare coupler knuckles to each side as shown in fig. 2.

The kit for the traction motor cables includes four castings: two sets of four stacked cables which go on the sides of the frame in front of the fuel tank as fig. 2 shows, and two sets of four bound cables which go behind the fuel tank.

Paint the frame and truck sideframes Engine Black. Paint the fuel gauge red, fuel sight glasses and fuel filler caps silver, and the spare coupler knuckles Rust.

I replaced the Athearn motor using a NorthWest Short Line repowering kit. Also, I installed constant-intensity directional headlights using a simple bridge rectifier circuit (from an article in the July 1991 MR) shown in fig. 3. I mounted this assembly on top of the motor with cyanoacrylate adhesive (CA) and used a pair of two-pin connectors to make connections with the body-mounted bulbs.

Body shell

Use a pin to make pilot marks at the lift rings and ends of the molded-on grab irons. Drill holes at these marks for new grabs and lift rings, then remove the molded-on details with a chisel-tip blade.

Drill mounting holes for the plows, uncoupling levers, m.u. hoses, bell, and horn. Remove the roof fans and radiator grill. I did this by twirling the point of a sharp hobby knife in each fan until a hole was made, then using the knife to carefully finish carving away material.

Remove the small access door in front of the dynamic brake grills, shown in fig. 2.

Remove the bottom half of the body-mounting rings below the walkway as shown in fig. 2. Fill the remaining half-circle with body putty and sand it smooth. This makes the side sills more realistic, but the body is no longer attached to the frame. The new motor fits snugly, though, and I've had no problems.

Use a razor saw to cut off the nose, cab, and cab sub-base. Assemble the new Cannon nose, cab, and sub-base. Glue them together as a subassembly, but don't add it to the body yet. Leave the windows out of the cab for now, and don't use the sunshade mounting strips.

Add the new radiator screens, fans, bell, lift rings, antenna, and horn.

The final step on the shell is to add the diamond tread plate to the walkway. This is a very thin, self-adhesive foil. To apply it, cut pieces a bit larger than needed, stick it on, and rub it vigorously with the plastic handle of a paintbrush to make sure it sticks well. Use a sharp hobby knife to trim around the edges of the walkways.

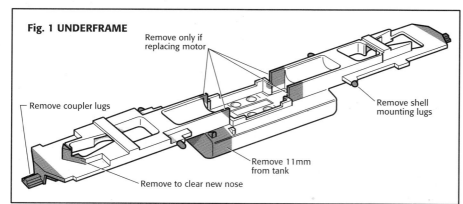

Fig. 1 UNDERFRAME

Remove only if replacing motor

Remove coupler lugs

Remove shell mounting lugs

Remove 11mm from tank

Remove to clear new nose

Jim Forbes

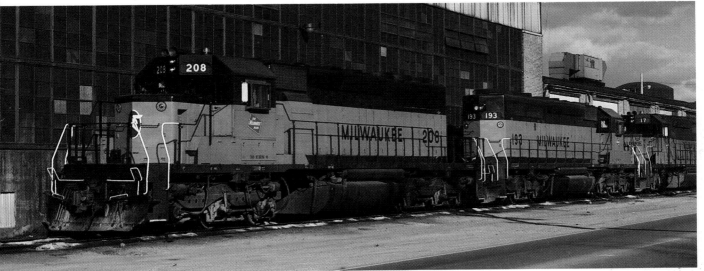

Gary W. Dolzall

Paint and decals

Badger's Accu-Flex is an extremely easy-to-use water-based paint. When trying it for the first time you may notice that it goes on heavy – perhaps even obscuring some of the fine detail. This is nothing to worry about because as it dries the excess paint seems to vanish, leaving a very smooth, even finish.

Another nice quality of this paint is that it dries in about 10 minutes – faster if you use a hair dryer. In fact, I masked this model, sprayed on two colors, and began applying decals all within an hour!

Wash all of the plastic parts in warm, soapy water to remove fingerprints and other oils. When the body is dry, spray it with Milwaukee Orange.

Follow the diagram on the Microscale decal sheet for masking the black lines and lightning stripe, then spray these areas with Engine Black.

Accu-Flex dries to a semi-gloss finish, ready for decals. I used Micro Sol setting solution and had no problems getting the decals to adhere to the paint. The builder's plates and other data came from Microscale set no. 87-48.

I followed the decals with a light coat of Floquil Flat Finish. This dries to a semi-gloss finish, and does an excellent job of hiding the edges of the decals.

The Milwaukee Road's final paint scheme, shown here on SD40-2s 208 and 193 in March 1985, featured the famous *Hiawatha* emblem on the nose.

Cab details

Number 195 had an all-weather window on the engineer's side. Paint the all-weather window Grimy Black and the window frames on the fireman's side silver.

I used four pieces of clear styrene for the front number boards. First I installed two clear pieces in the openings. After painting the other two black and adding decal numbers, I installed them behind the clear material.

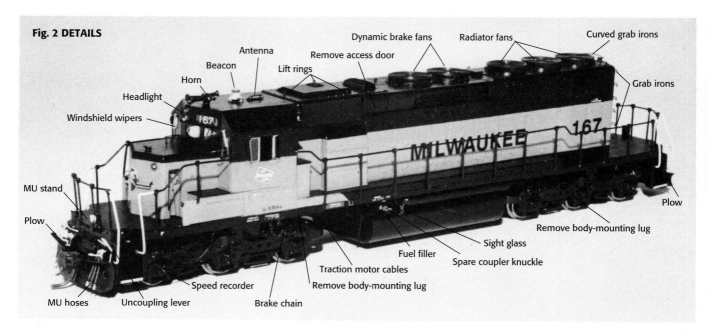

Fig. 2 DETAILS

Windshield wipers · Headlight · Horn · Beacon · Antenna · Lift rings · Remove access door · Dynamic brake fans · Radiator fans · Curved grab irons · Grab irons · Plow · Remove body-mounting lug · Sight glass · Spare coupler knuckle · Fuel filler · Traction motor cables · Remove body-mounting lug · Brake chain · Uncoupling lever · Speed recorder · MU hoses · Plow · MU stand

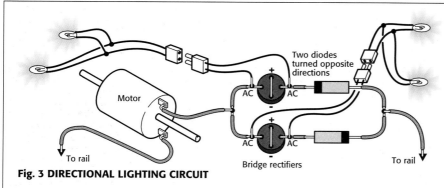

Motor · To rail · AC AC · + − · AC AC · + − · Bridge rectifiers · Two diodes turned opposite directions · To rail

Fig. 3 DIRECTIONAL LIGHTING CIRCUIT

Hiawatha-scheme SD40-2s

The following units had the *Hiawatha* lightning-stripe scheme: 130, 142, 144, 148, 149, 151, 157, 159, 164, 166-168, 175, 183, 184, 188-190, 192-195, 197, 201, 204-206, 208, and 209

Finish the cab by adding the windshield wipers, painted silver, and the headlight casting. Drill no. 56 holes into the front and rear headlight castings and add the Miniatronics light bulbs. Use CA to secure these parts.

Final details

I trimmed the stanchions on the front and rear decks to mount in holes on the walkway, as the photos show. Add a drop of CA to the top of each stanchion to hold the railings tight. Brush-paint the handrails black with white at the corners and paint the step faces, uncoupling levers, and plow grab irons white.

Glue the air filter in place, then add air lines by running .020" wire from the air tanks through the filter and up to the bottom of the walkway as shown in the color photo. Secure with CA.

Use a fine-point black magic marker to color the gasket around the water-sight glass on the engineer's side of the long hood. Then fill the hole with Microscale Micro Kristal Klear.

Add the m.u. hoses, painted Grimy Black with silver tips, and add the plows to both ends and secure them with CA. I used Kadee no. 5 couplers in their own boxes with the mounting ears trimmed.

My SD40-2 is now ready to go into service on the Milwaukee Road's hotshot *Sprint* intermodal trains. ✿

Bill of materials

Accu-Flex paints
16-01 Engine Black
16-02 Reefer White
16-03 Grimy Black
16-05 Weathered Black
16-42 Milwaukee Orange

A-Line
29200 windshield wipers

Athearn
4400 SD40-2 undecorated

Cannon & Co.
1103 81" low nose
1202 cab sub-base
1404 radiator grills
1501 Dash-2 cab kit

Custom Finishing
253 headlight

Detail Associates
1505 m.u. stand
1508 m.u. hoses
1803 antenna
2202 grab irons
2206 lift rings

2211 uncoupling lever
2301 all-weather window
2310 wind deflector
2807 speed recorder
3101 fuel gauge
6503 curved grab iron

Details West
106 rotary beacon
129 bell
139 air filter
150 plow (rear)
155 plow (front)
166 fuel filler
172 cab step lights
190 horn
195 buffer plate
196 spare knuckle/bracket
224 traction motor cables

Floquil
110015 Flat Finish

K&S Engineering
499 .020" wire

Microscale
MI-2 Micro Sol

MI-9 Micro Kristal Klear
87-48 diesel data decals
87-441 Milwaukee Road *Hiawatha*-scheme diesel decals

Miniatronics
18-001-10 1.5-volt subminiature light bulbs

NorthWest Short Line
1634 Athearn SD40-2 repower kit
71414 40" nickel-plated wheelsets

Precision Scale Co.
3932 dynamic brake fans
3966 radiator fans (2 pkgs.)
48237 chain

Radio Shack
276-1152 bridge rectifiers (2)
276-1101 diodes

Wm. K. Walthers
166-1 diamond tread plate

Detailing a Rio Grande Tunnel Motor

Superdetails to enhance an Athearn HO scale SD40T-2

BY DAVID A. BONTRAGER
PHOTOS BY THE AUTHOR

ONE OF MY main goals as a model railroader has been to try and capture in HO scale what my favorite prototype, the Denver and Rio Grande Western, does with its diesel locomotives and rolling stock. If you model present-day railroads you know that a goal like this never leaves you unchallenged. In the February Paint Shop I explained how I built a model of a D&RGW modernized waycar. Now I'll move up to the head end.

As this article describes, reproducing a Rio Grande "Tunnel Motor" required a lot of careful modeling. But I was determined to build a scale model of this unique variation of the popular EMD SD40-2 heavy-duty road diesel. Follow my construction and detailing suggestions, and you can have one with less work than you might have thought.

THE PROTOTYPE

What's been nicknamed Tunnel Motor is properly referred to as an SD40T-2. This road diesel was built to cope with the radiator cooling problems caused by extended heavy-load operation through tunnels in the Sierra Nevadas and the Rockies. Unlike their normal cousins, SD40T-2s have radiator systems arranged to draw cool air from the lower portion of the tunnel. This keeps hot exhaust gases near the ceiling, away from the radiators, so the cooling system works better.

Only two railroads own Tunnel Motors: the Denver & Rio Grande Western and the Southern Pacific. However, as Robert Zenk pointed out in the January 1985 MODEL RAILROADER, these units have made their way all over the country. That's why, as he mentioned, you can realistically include one on your layout even if you aren't modeling the Rio Grande or Southern Pacific. In his article Bob explained the SP units in detail. Rather than repeat his great modeling hints, I will simply cover the methods I used to add D&RGW detailing to a factory-painted Athearn HO scale SD40T-2.

First, though, a little more information about these diesels. According to the second edition of Charles W. McDonald's book *Diesel Locomotive Rosters: U. S., Canada, and Mexico* (Kalmbach Publishing Co., 1986), the Rio Grande owns 73 SD40T-2 locomotives numbered 5341-5413. Number 5367, shown in fig. 1, is typical of these locomotives.

While the D&RGW units are all 3000-hp locomotives equipped about the same, there are a few minor differences here and there. For example, one order has the lower front headlights mounted on a strange looking box rather than set into the nose in the usual manner (fig. 2). These units are numbered 5386-5397,

Fig. 1. Above: 5367 is typical of the Denver & Rio Grande Western's SD40T-2 Tunnel Motors. It has the walkway-level air intake grids at the rear and the snowplow and low-nose headlight arrangement on the short hood. **Fig. 2. Right:** Unique details, like this boxy low hood headlight mount on units 5386-5397, are easy to do with bits of styrene. They add a nice bit of variation if more units are built.

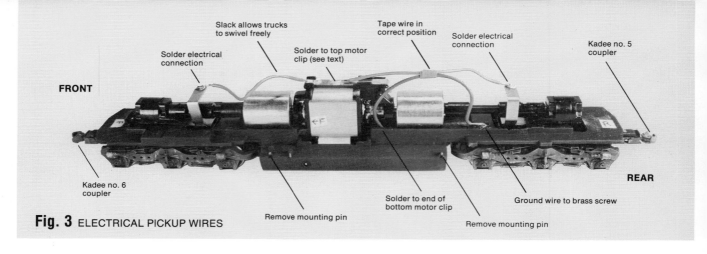

Fig. 3 ELECTRICAL PICKUP WIRES

Labels (clockwise): Slack allows trucks to swivel freely · Tape wire in correct position · Solder electrical connection · Kadee no. 5 coupler · Solder to top motor clip (see text) · Solder electrical connection · FRONT · REAR · Kadee no. 6 coupler · Remove mounting pin · Solder to end of bottom motor clip · Remove mounting pin · Ground wire to brass screw

according to Joseph A. Strapac's book *Rio Grande Diesels, A Pictorial History: Vol. 2* (Shade Tree Books, 1984). This would be an interesting variation to model using a piece of styrene. However, I'll deal only with units that have the standard headlight arrangement.

APPROACH TO MODELING

My philosophy on detailing is to add enough to capture the overall look of the prototype without changing every bit of detail. I never add anything that could hinder the operation of a model, nor will I risk removing something that may be vital to good performance. Reliable operation takes priority over detail.

To reduce the risk of breaking details, I build my locomotives so the body sits on the frame. It can be removed by lifting rather than prying it off. This is accomplished by removing the factory mounting pins (shown in fig. 3), permanently mounting the plow on the pilot, and leaving a space under the rear coupler.

The prototype Rio Grande Tunnel Motors have fuel tanks that are shorter than what is cast on the Athearn model. I kept the cast-on length because it doesn't distract from the overall appearance. The sand pipes are not included on this particular unit, so they were also excluded from my model.

As a final way of simplifying what I'd have to do, I used a factory-painted model. That may not appeal to all of you. So if you decide to use an undecorated shell, I'd recommend painting it

gloss black and applying decals in the usual manner. Rio Grande SD40T-2s all use the jumbo lettering on the sides and have the small "Rio Grande" on the front of the low hood.

REWORKING THE CHASSIS

On road locomotives I use the stock Athearn motor and fine-tune the chassis. The Athearn chassis usually operate well right out of the box, so it takes only a little effort to obtain top performance.

I begin by marking the frame and truck assemblies "F" (front) and "R" (rear) for easy reference. A small screwdriver works well to gently pry off the sideframes and worm housings, but be careful not to lose the small bronze end bearings and the thin washers from the worm gear shaft. It's also a good idea to keep everything organized to prevent misplacing any small parts.

After both trucks are out, I remove the motor and check the frame using a metal ruler to be sure it's not bent or twisted. A bent frame is rare, but adjustments can be made by hand. Then I put the trucks back in the frame and check to make sure it sits level. If necessary, adjust the metal tabs on the trucks to level the frame (see fig. 4).

Once again, I remove both truck assemblies and use a small screwdriver to disengage the gearbox clips so the axles and gears can be taken apart. Factory oil can be removed by washing the parts (except the motor) in rubbing alcohol.

Checking the motor's end play is next.

It has to have adequate end play to operate without binding, so I don't get too concerned about it unless things are just plain sloppy. NorthWest Short Line sells thrust washers (part no. 103-4) that may be added next to the Athearn thrust washers to remove excess end play.

Figure 3 shows how I add electrical pickup wires to the motor. To avoid losing the motor brushes or springs, I do one side at a time and make sure the brushes are reinstalled so their curved ends match the contour of the commutator.

Once the truck parts are dry, I inspect the gears for burrs and flash, removing any with a hobby knife or small file. Then I install the gears (dry) and turn the gear train by hand to make sure everything works smoothly. Then I remove the gears, apply LaBelle no. 106 plastic-compatible grease to the gear shafts, and reinstall the gears with a spot of grease at each point where they mesh.

WHEELSETS AND COUPLERS

For improved electrical pickup I rely on NorthWest Short Line's nickel-silver wheelsets. Number 71424 (scale 42" diameter) matches the stock Athearn wheel size, while no. 71414 (scale 40") matches the prototype size. To install them you must first remove the stock wheelsets from the axle gears. I hold a wheel/axle assembly in both hands and twist the wheels in opposite directions while I pull them apart. Then I install the new wheels using the same twisting action while I push them into the gear assembly

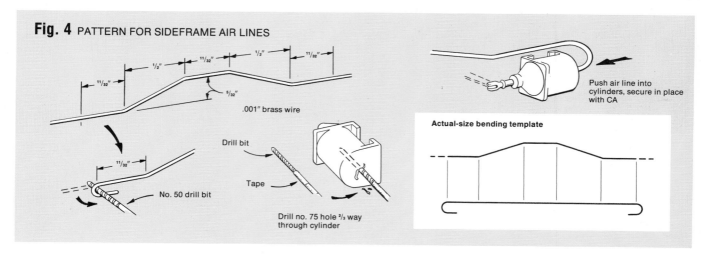

Fig. 4 PATTERN FOR SIDEFRAME AIR LINES

.001" brass wire · No. 50 drill bit · Drill bit · Tape · Drill no. 75 hole ⅔ way through cylinder · Push air line into cylinders, secure in place with CA · Actual-size bending template

Dimensions: ¹¹⁄₃₂" · ½" · ¹¹⁄₃₂" · ½" · ¹¹⁄₃₂" · ⁵⁄₃₂" · ¹¹⁄₃₂"

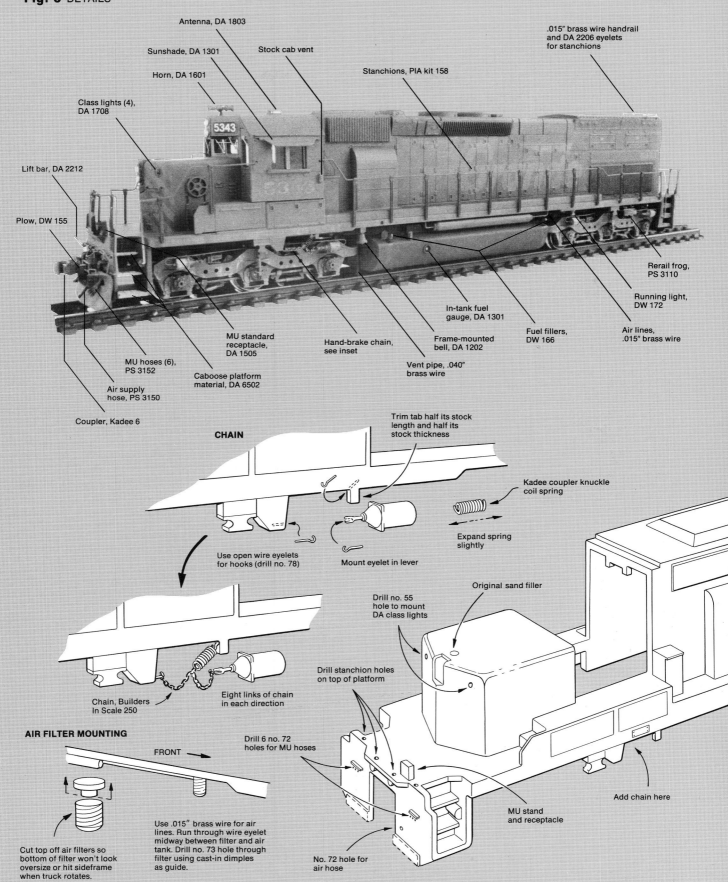

Fig. 5 DETAILS

Antenna, DA 1803

Sunshade, DA 1301

Horn, DA 1601

Stock cab vent

Stanchions, PIA kit 158

.015" brass wire handrail and DA 2206 eyelets for stanchions

Class lights (4), DA 1708

5343

Lift bar, DA 2212

Plow, DW 155

Rerail frog, PS 3110

In-tank fuel gauge, DA 1301

Running light, DW 172

Fuel fillers, DW 166

Air lines, .015" brass wire

MU standard receptacle, DA 1505

Hand-brake chain, see inset

Frame-mounted bell, DA 1202

MU hoses (6), PS 3152

Caboose platform material, DA 6502

Vent pipe, .040" brass wire

Air supply hose, PS 3150

Coupler, Kadee 6

CHAIN

Trim tab half its stock length and half its stock thickness

Kadee coupler knuckle coil spring

Use open wire eyelets for hooks (drill no. 78)

Mount eyelet in lever

Expand spring slightly

Original sand filler

Drill no. 55 hole to mount DA class lights

Chain, Builders In Scale 250

Eight links of chain in each direction

Drill stanchion holes on top of platform

AIR FILTER MOUNTING

FRONT

Drill 6 no. 72 holes for MU hoses

Add chain here

Cut top off air filters so bottom of filter won't look oversize or hit sideframe when truck rotates.

Use .015" brass wire for air lines. Run through wire eyelet midway between filter and air tank. Drill no. 73 hole through filter using cast-in dimples as guide.

No. 72 hole for air hose

MU stand and receptacle

(making sure to include the tiny bronze bearings). The stub axles must not touch each other inside the gear, or they will cause a short circuit.

Next, I adjust the gears so they are centered between the wheels without binding the bearings. I also check the wheel spacing with an NMRA gauge and make any final adjustments. When I reinstall the wheel/axle assemblies in the truck, I make sure the bearings are properly set, apply Labelle no. 106 grease to the gears, and snap the retainer plates in place. As a final check, I push the truck assembly back and forth on a piece of track. They will not roll on their own, but each truck should push easily without binding of any kind.

For couplers I decided to use the long Kadee no. 6 on the front end so the unit can be coupled to any car or locomotive without interference between their uncoupling pins and the SD40T-2's snowplow. This is especially helpful if the locomotive operates on a club layout.

I filed the mounting pad and used .010″ plastic shims to level and adjust the coupler height. When everything was satisfactory, I removed the couplers and lightly spray-painted them a dirty rusty color. After the paint had dried, I applied Kadee's Greas-em dry lubricant to the knuckle pivot points and operated the coupler by hand until the knuckle moved freely. Then I set the couplers aside for final installation later on.

FUEL TANKS AND SIDEFRAMES

Now I was ready to add some of the details that transformed this into a realistic model of a unique prototype. Installing details usually involves drilling tiny holes in the plastic frame. To make this step a bit easier, I created a special tool by mounting a needle in a ¼″ dowel. I used this to mark the starting point for small drill bits in plastic.

The fuel tank and truck sideframe details I added are shown in figs. 3 and 4. I filed any burrs and flash on the fuel tank and frame casting before adding details. Next, I sprayed the frame, fuel tank, and sideframes with Floquil Engine Black and then a light coat of Floquil Weathered Black. I kept the paint spray almost dry on the bare plastic sideframes to prevent etching them and destroying the delicate EMD logo.

I weathered the fuel tank with Floquil Grime and dirt colors (light brown or tan) thinned about 4:1 thinner to paint. I applied a light spray on the sides of the fuel tank and a little heavier coat on the ends. My sideframes got a light application of rust and light gray with an almost dry paintbrush. Satisfied with the paint and weathering, I sprayed everything with Testor's Dullcote. Later, I added fuel spills around the fuel fillers using a small brush and thinned gloss black. I also painted the outside face of the nickel-silver wheels with flat black.

I installed the motor next, putting a small drop of clipper oil on each truck pivot point and installing the truck assemblies. I used Labelle no. 108 oil and applied as small a drop as possible where the bronze bearings ride on the worm gear shaft. Being careful to properly

align the worm gear bearings in each housing, I added Labelle no. 106 grease in several grooves of the worm gear and snapped the retainer housing into place.

The motor lead wires must be trimmed to a length that allows both trucks to swivel freely. I tinned the wire ends and soldered them so the top wires went to the top tabs on the trucks and the bottom wire went to the brass pin in the frame. I made sure the bottom wire was next to the motor so the body would slip over it, but still not touch any moving parts. The photo in fig. 3 shows my finished chassis before its final test run.

I installed the sideframes by carefully pressing them into place. If they go on hard (due to paint buildup), I'd advise lubricating the mounting tabs with Testor's paint thinner.

I turned the chassis upside down and used wood blocks at each end so it could not roll over. The speed recorder cable was installed next, using a length that doesn't let it sag when the truck is sitting straight and level. While the engine was inverted, I also put on the couplers, making sure the screws were tight yet didn't hinder the coupler's operation. Then I applied a drop of cyanoacrylate adhesive (CA) to the head of each screw to keep them from vibrating loose.

Test-running the chassis with everything in place tells me if there is any binding. I let it run for a while to break everything in. With no load, a chassis like this should draw around ¼ ampere.

THE CAB AND BODY

Whenever I detail a plastic carbody like this SD40T-2, I wind up with unused holes to fill. I recommend Bondo Glazing and Spot Putty no. 907 for this filling work as it dries fast, has little shrinkage, easily sands smooth, accepts paint very well, can be used on plastic, and comes in a tube. I used this material to fill the unused holes (shown in fig. 5) originally designed for the end stanchions and body-mounting system. Any areas where filler was sanded were touched up with Floquil D&RGW Orange. Even if it isn't a perfect match, I don't worry about it as the weathering covers up any variation.

I separated the cab from the body and trimmed off its mounting tabs as I prefer to cement the cab in place. Then I prepared the cab details shown in fig. 5, but didn't permanently mount anything at this time. Moving on, I painted the front number boards white, allowed them to dry, and applied number decals from a Microscale set. If you use numbers from a Herald King set, the front number boards should be painted black.

The original headlight lenses must be modified so the MV Products lenses will fit. I cut off the rounded face of the Athearn lenses and sanded the shank until it slipped into the mounting holes easily with a slight friction fit. Then I inserted the modified lens partway, leaving a recess to receive the MV lenses, and cemented the plastic lenses in place with Micro Weld. While the cement dried, I cut new window material to fit the cab windows. I set them aside for later installation, as I did the MV lenses.

Mounting the cab on the body can be quite a project if you happen to get a body that's warped. I used a rubber band as a clamp and let the joint cure under pressure overnight (a day or two would have been better).

Before setting the body on the frame, I trimmed the rear bracket for the hand-brake spring. This allows the truck to rotate without fouling the air line on the sideframe. Figure 5 shows how I made the hand-brake spring using a Kadee coil spring, even though the spring is oversized and has blunt ends.

SNOWPLOW AND SAFETY CHAIN

After checking one more time that the body fit all the way down on the frame, I was ready to mount the snowplow. Look at figs. 6 and 7 to see how I did it. Mounting the plow .060″ above the rails may seem extremely high, but I've found this looks fine on the finished model. It's also less likely to catch on trackside obstructions that might be too high or too close to the track, especially on curved tracks due to the plow's overhang.

The prototype SD40T-2 has the openings in the plow face for m.u. hoses, but the trap doors are gone. To simulate this I removed the cast doors from the Details West snowplow and filed the area to a smooth contour as shown in fig. 7. The doors should be left alone for a more typical D&RGW unit.

Precision Investment Associates (PIA) makes a stanchion set that adds a nice touch to the SD40T-2 model, so the additional work of bending the handrails was worth it. I had extra .015″ brass wire handy in case I made an error. The kit instructions explain the assembly and installation procedure adequately, so I don't need to say more. I should note that I didn't make one solid handrail across the ends as PIA suggests (also like the Athearn handrails), because I wanted to add the safety chain details.

For those details I began by drilling out the stanchion mounting holes to allow the pins to slip into the body casting with only slight pressure. This reduced the possibility of accidental damage during final assembly. I used the Athearn handrails and PIA stanchions, along with photos of the prototype, as guides when I bent the new handrails. As each assembly was completed, I removed it and placed it with the other parts that were to be painted black.

FINAL DETAILS

I had just a few more details to add, starting with the installation of the lower headlight assembly (fig. 6). I began by filing the bracket mounting area flat. I continued by making a series of light cuts with a modified X-acto chisel knife blade, starting a little on the narrow side and slowly trimming it to exact size using the casting as a guide.

Changing unit numbers meant first removing the factory numbers by applying Scalecoat paint remover to each digit with a very small brush. I was careful to avoid getting any paint remover on the black paint. After a few minutes, I made a second light application and worked it around with the brush. Then I wiped off

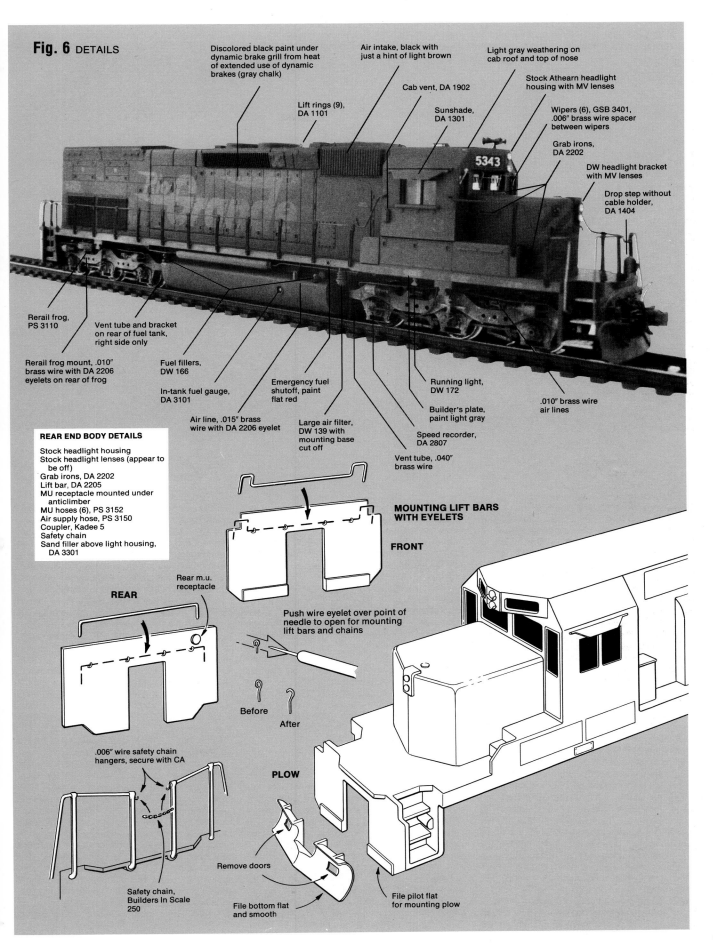

Fig. 6 DETAILS

Discolored black paint under dynamic brake grill from heat of extended use of dynamic brakes (gray chalk)

Air intake, black with just a hint of light brown

Light gray weathering on cab roof and top of nose

Cab vent, DA 1902

Stock Athearn headlight housing with MV lenses

Lift rings (9), DA 1101

Sunshade, DA 1301

Wipers (6), GSB 3401, .006" brass wire spacer between wipers

Grab irons, DA 2202

DW headlight bracket with MV lenses

Drop step without cable holder, DA 1404

Rerail frog, PS 3110

Vent tube and bracket on rear of fuel tank, right side only

Rerail frog mount, .010" brass wire with DA 2206 eyelets on rear of frog

Fuel fillers, DW 166

In-tank fuel gauge, DA 3101

Emergency fuel shutoff, paint flat red

Running light, DW 172

.010" brass wire air lines

Air line, .015" brass wire with DA 2206 eyelet

Large air filter, DW 139 with mounting base cut off

Builder's plate, paint light gray

Speed recorder, DA 2807

Vent tube, .040" brass wire

REAR END BODY DETAILS

Stock headlight housing
Stock headlight lenses (appear to be off)
Grab irons, DA 2202
Lift bar, DA 2205
MU receptacle mounted under anticlimber
MU hoses (6), PS 3152
Air supply hose, PS 3150
Coupler, Kadee 5
Safety chain
Sand filler above light housing, DA 3301

MOUNTING LIFT BARS WITH EYELETS

FRONT

REAR

Rear m.u. receptacle

Push wire eyelet over point of needle to open for mounting lift bars and chains

Before

After

.006" wire safety chain hangers, secure with CA

PLOW

Safety chain, Builders In Scale 250

Remove doors

File bottom flat and smooth

File pilot flat for mounting plow

75

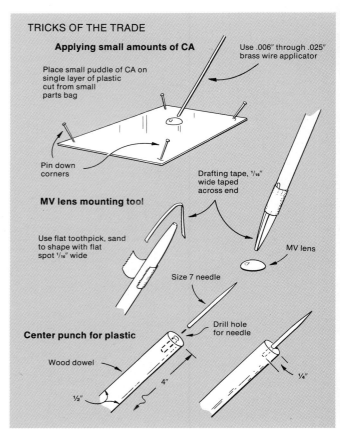

Applying small amounts of CA

Use .006" through .025" brass wire applicator

Place small puddle of CA on single layer of plastic cut from small parts bag

Pin down corners

Drafting tape, 1/16" wide taped across end

MV lens mounting tool

Use flat toothpick, sand to shape with flat spot 1/16" wide

Size 7 needle

MV lens

Drill hole for needle

Center punch for plastic

Wood dowel

1/2"

4"

1/4"

Fig. 7. Left: With all the additional front end details in place, the author's weathered model takes on the characteristic appearance of its prototype.

the area with a wet paper towel. The numbers had begun to fade, though more applications were needed to get them to disappear. Finally, I rubbed the area with an eraser to smooth everything out.

An application of Floquil Hi-Gloss came next, then I let the model dry. On small areas like this, a brush would do fine, but I tried to cover an area up to a joint or seam so there was no noticeable starting point. Once the paint had dried, I applied the new decal numbers in the usual manner and finished with a spray coat of Dullcote. I didn't worry about minor differences in color between the renumbered areas and the body paint as weathering blended everything.

Another detail that makes a model diesel look more realistic is open tread steps. I fabricated these from Detail Associates caboose platform material that I was careful not to bend. With a sharp hobby knife I cut it on a hard, flat surface to obtain clean cuts and reduce filing. Then I sprayed the grids silver before installing them. This material didn't produce an accurate locomotive step, but did give an effective open step appearance. To further the see-through effect, I painted the edges of the body step silver but left the top surface black. When the treads were in place, the grids appeared to be open clear through.

Lastly, I painted a 1/8" x 1/4" piece of .010" plastic black and cemented it behind the water sight glass opening. I used Athearn's stock plastic headlight lenses

to represent rear lights that are turned off. As for grab irons, I didn't shave off the cast-on ones, because I've found that once the Detail Associates grabs are on they nicely conceal the originals. However, I did shave off the molded tabs so I could replace the lift rings.

WEATHERING

Rio Grande locomotives come in a variety of blacks and grays, depending on how long it's been since their last washing and how many trips they've made through the front range tunnel district. With that in mind, I masked off the air intakes and weathered my model to the road's mostly black color with just a hint of light brown or tan. I sprayed it Floquil Engine Black, followed by a light dusting of Floquil Earth mixed 6 parts thinner to 1 part paint.

I continued the weathering to give this model a grayish look by mixing 1 part Floquil Weathered Black with 4 parts Dio-Sol. Then I airbrushed the entire body and any unattached parts with several light coats to give the locomotive an overall dirty look. For a heavier weathering job and a blacker appearance, I use Floquil Engine Black.

Next, I dusted some light gray chalk on the roof, sunshades, and top of the low hood. I work the chalk with a foam cosmetic pad, then fan it out with a dry, soft-bristle brush. It takes some care to keep from overdoing it as chalk on flat Floquil paint doesn't neutralize as much

as it will on smooth or glossy paint. I set the chalk with a spray of Dullcote.

Final touching up and fine drybrush weathering were done after all the details were in place. A little rust and dirt were added here and there on the handrails, stanchions, and small parts around the lower portions of the body. Then I used a dry, medium-size brush to do additional heavy weathering on the pilots, side sills, and snowplow.

To simulate the exhaust soot on top of the unit, I mixed 1 part Floquil Engine Black with 3 parts Dio-Sol and sprayed it on top of the body. It took a little practice for me to achieve the desired effect, but the soot pattern should fan out the farther it gets from the exhaust outlet. I began spraying close in at the exhaust port and then moved the airbrush up and away to fan out the spray pattern. It's important to keep the airbrush moving throughout this step to prevent overloading one area. I laid a lightweight, plastic sandwich bag over the low hood to protect the front from the overspray.

After installing the MV headlight lenses and filling the sight glass opening with clear epoxy, I stood back and admired my model. While the detailing I did may seem like a lot of work, I've found that the process has become a very enjoyable hobby activity. It's especially rewarding when I watch my finished Tunnel Motor begin its next climb up the front range of the Rockies en route to Salt Lake City. ✿

Allan Houghton modeled this GATX MP15 after one of three units now in service on the StL&A.

Modeling a GATX Leasing MP15 in HO scale

An easy project that would be at home on any contempory layout

BY ALLAN N. HOUGHTON
PHOTOS BY THE AUTHOR

The St. Lawrence & Atlantic RR (StL&A) began leasing three EMD MP15s from GATX in January 1991. [The author's feature on modeling the StL&A appeared in the February 1992 issue of *Model Railroader* Magazine.—Ed.] Locomotive leasing is an alternative to ownership and a means of trying out equipment to see if a model is suitable for purchase. General American Transportation Corp. (GATX) is one of several firms in the leasing business, and their locomotives can be found on large and small railroads throughout the United States.

The StL&A's three leased locomotives, nos. 9625-9627, work in both road and switching service. They're ex-Conrail, as evidenced by the spot painting around the GATX logo. A model of such a unit would fit in well on most contemporary railroads, as leased units can show up on any railroad short of power.

Modeling

I used a Con-Cor HO scale Conrail MP15 for my model. This turned out to be appropriate, as the Con-Cor model wears no. 9626. A "quickie" job would be to paint out the Conrail logo, retain the number, and letter the model for GATX. However, there were several detail differences I wanted to correct.

The most noticeable difference is the number of cab windows. The prototype GATX MP15s have two fewer windows in the cab sides and one less in the rear. The units also have a paper air filter box atop the hood, and their front sandboxes are enlarged.

I began by using an X-acto knife to trim away the moldings around the windows that are to be blocked off. As fig. 1 shows, I removed a scale 7'-1"-long section from the hood to make way for the air filter box. You'll want to pop off the exhaust stacks while cutting the hood. Next, cut the horn-mounting lug off the cab roof.

Assemble the filter box as shown in fig. 1. You can also make the sandbox extensions and fill in the cab windows as shown in fig. 2. The only problem I had with these modifications involved fitting the tops of the sandbox extensions against the hood. If necessary, use contour putty to smooth these joints. [Bowser offers auxiliary sandboxes as part no. 13-426 in its Cary Locomotive Works line.—Ed.]

Cut the largest horn from the three-chime unit provided and glue it to the

Bill of materials

Accu-cals decals
5820 B&M, MEC switchers
5836 CV, GT, CN, DW&P diesels

Con-Cor
1-1557 Conrail MP15

Detail Associates
1401 drop step
1506 m.u. stand
1508 m.u. hoses
1803 antenna
2212 uncoupling lever

Evergreen styrene
9005 .010" clear sheet
9009 .005" plain sheet
9020 .020" plain sheet

Floquil paint
110010 Engine Black
110011 Reefer White
110013 Grimy Black
110058 Conrail Blue

Herald King decal
B1620 Berlin Mills Ry. boxcar

Kadee
7 couplers

Testor
1260 Dullcote spray
1261 Glosscote spray

Walthers decals
934-D683 diesel data set
936-D606 boxcar data set

Woodland Scenics
DT507 white Gothic dry transfers

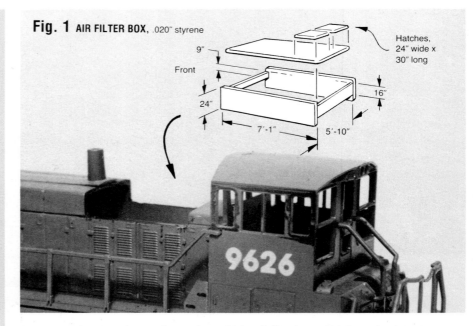

Fig. 1 AIR FILTER BOX, .020" styrene

Remove the hood section as shown, then add the air filter box, which is made of .020" styrene.

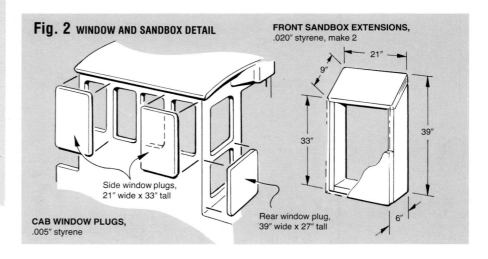

Fig. 2 WINDOW AND SANDBOX DETAIL

FRONT SANDBOX EXTENSIONS, .020" styrene, make 2

CAB WINDOW PLUGS, .005" styrene

Side window plugs, 21" wide x 33" tall

Rear window plug, 39" wide x 27" tall

cab front, centered over the windows. Snap the exhaust stacks back into place, and install the bell and the rear sandbox filler caps.

Painting

I followed the prototype's lead and just spot-painted my model, although I also had to paint the new plastic parts. I used Floquil Conrail Blue, applied with a no. 5 brush. It took two coats to hide the Conrail herald. Naturally, since I didn't care if this spot-painting showed, it didn't.

Between coats of blue, I installed the pilot details as shown in fig. 3. Use a .025" drill for the m.u. hose holes. Paint the m.u. stand and the drop step blue when applying the second coat to the body.

Another job to tackle while the blue dries is to paint the railings at the steps white. You can install the end railings at any time, but leave the two side (long) railings and the four short railings (for the cab steps and rear platform) off for now.

When you've finished the blue, brushpaint the walkways and platforms with Floquil Engine Black. Touch up any blue areas, paint the number boards black, and seal the paint with Testor's Glosscote.

Lettering

Finding decals took longer than expected, and I ended up using bits and pieces left over from other projects. [Microscale has since come out with set no. 87-557, GATX locomotives, containing the GATX logo, "LEASING CORPORATION" lettering, and numbers.— Ed.] Most of the pieces are generic, and many sets other than the ones I used contain lettering that will work (check your decal files and scraps).

The "GATX" is from a Woodland Scenics no. DT507 white Gothic dry-transfer set (3⁄16" letters). The photos show how the four letters run together. Spacing the G against the A isn't a problem, but the top of the T is a little too short to reach the A and the X. Applying a little Reefer White with a no. 0 brush made up the difference. The DT507 set also provided the "GCCX" below the cab windows. Use the 1⁄16" size.

Next, I took care of the "LEASING CORPORATION" block. The "LEAS" and "CORPORATION" came from Herald King's no. B1620 set, the "ING" from a word in the Walthers no. 936-D606 boxcar data set. In applying these I found they sagged into the space between the second and third access doors. With clarity in mind, I cut the decal film to spread the word "corporation" on one side, "leasing" on the other.

Fig. 3 DETAILS

- Antenna
- Wind deflectors
- Air filter box
- Sandbox extensions, both sides
- Drop step
- MU stand
- Uncoupling lever
- MU hoses

A Walthers no. 934-D683 diesel data set provided the "MP15," although you'll have to get each figure from a different part of the sheet. The same set provided the numbers for the number boards. The six red-and-white "DANGER" labels are from Accu-cals set no. 5836. The set has two each of 150-, 300-, 450-, and 600-volt labels. The prototype MP15 labels are 600 volts, but don't worry too much about this—you can't read much more than "DANGER" without a magnifying glass. Note that the air filter box has two labels on each side, while the cab is labeled on the fireman's side only.

The only lettering that I couldn't duplicate is the block on the side of the rear sandboxes, which should read "OWNED BY GATX CAPITAL CORPORATION" Visible just behind the cab on the prototype photo). I fudged this by using similar plates from Accu-cals set no. 5820H. I turned them upside down, too, so it's harder to read "Boston & Maine Equipment Trust."

I gave the lowest step on each platform a white edge, then weathered the model slightly by drybrushing it with Floquil Grimy Black. In "drybrushing,"

you dip your brush in the paint, then wipe off most of the paint on a paper towel. When the brush is almost dry, brush it across the model. The result is a grimy, streaked appearance. If you haven't tried drybrushing before, practice on some scrap material before doing it on a model.

Not only did I dirty the body, I hit the truck sideframes and fuel tank as well. Then I added two coats of Dullcote.

Final Assembly

Snap the cab off the hood, and install the windows and rear headlight lens. With the cab on, install the remaining handrails and the front headlight lens. The three StL&A units are equipped with wind deflectors on both sides of the cab. I simulated these with .010" clear styrene. I cut four rectangles a scale 6" wide and 24" tall and simply glued them to the cab.

I replaced the horn-hook couplers with a set of Kadee no. 7 couplers. The mounting screw wouldn't tighten properly on the new coupler box, but I solved this problem by adding a U-shaped shim of .005" styrene between the coupler box and the washer under the screwhead. A drop of cement secured the shim.

Snapping the body shell onto the chassis completes this locomotive. This is my second StL&A engine in paint schemes that cover 9 of that short line's 11 engines. I'm not done yet!

The author took this photograph of GATX MP15 no. 9626 at Island Pond, Vt., in March of 1991.

Illinois Central's new black scheme

A simple but attractive scheme that makes an ideal project for beginners

BY MIKE LORD
PHOTOS BY THE AUTHOR

*A*N OLD NAME in railroading re-emerged in 1988, as the Illinois Central Gulf RR became the Illinois Central. This name change also brought a color scheme change. After several years of ICG orange-and-gray and orange-and-white diesels, a basic black scheme (similar to that worn by early IC diesels) became standard. The new black scheme is simple but attractive, and the simplicity of Mike Lord's project makes it an ideal one for beginners.

FOLLOWING the Illinois Central's emergence as a separate entity and the reintroduction of a black paint scheme for locomotives, I decided to model one of their units. I saw a GP38-2 in the new scheme going through Tuscola, Ill., and thought it would be an appropriate prototype to model.

I chose no. 9567 since its various components closely match Athearn's HO scale GP38-2 model (type-M trucks and medium fuel tank). This locomotive is one of 15 ex-Gulf, Mobile & Ohio GP38-2s, numbered 9560-9574. Units 9560, 9562, and 9570 are out of service.

The Athearn shell requires only a few modifications. The cab has a flat vent on the left-hand side below the windows. To remove this I used an X-acto no. 17 blade and fine wet-or-dry sandpaper.

Since these particular units have flat pilots, the next step is to remove the footboards from the bottom of the Athearn pilots. I sawed these off using a fine-tooth saw and a file. Then I added a piece of .010″ styrene across the pilot and filed the edges to the correct shape. Once it was in place I added a scrap piece of thicker styrene across the back for stability.

Because the styrene piece goes across the entire width of the pilot, I had to body-mount the couplers. To do this using Kadee no. 5 couplers, I had to create a coupler-mounting pad behind the pilot. I used four layers of Evergreen .060″ x .250″ strip styrene, glued in the cavity under the end walkway, to get the correct coupler height. Using the Kadee coupler pocket as a guide, I drilled and tapped a hole in the new mounting pad to accept a 2-56 screw. The couplers were installed later because the coupler-mounting lugs on the Athearn frame also had to be removed.

Next, I assembled the handrails on the shell by pressing the railings and stanchions into the body, then gluing the stanchions to the railings with CA. After the glue had dried I removed the assemblies from the shell.

The bill of materials and fig. 1 show the details I added. The only details I didn't attach before painting were the handrails, windshield wipers, and two grab irons on the nose (these would get in the way of the nose herald). I did, however, drill the holes for the grab irons before painting.

Bill of materials

Athearn
4612 GP38-2, without dynamic brakes

Detail Associates
1202 bell
1301 cab sunshade
1402 drop step
1505 m.u. stand
1508 m.u. hoses
1801 antenna
2202 grab irons
2212 uncoupling levers
2807 speed recorder
6503 curved grab irons
101101 lift rings

Evergreen styrene
159 .060" x .250" strip
9010 .010" sheet

Kadee
5 couplers

Microscale decal
87-528 Illinois Central diesels 1988

MV Products
LS-25 lenses

Pactra
2140 Crystal Clear spray

Precision Scale Co.
3968 windshield wipers

Scalecoat II paint
2001 Loco Black
2074 Loco Grime

Testor
1260 Dullcote spray
1749 Model Master Flat Black
1768 Model Master Flat White
1781 Model Master Aluminum

Utah Pacific
60 horn

G. Sires; Jim Shepard collection
Ex-Gulf, Mobile & Ohio GP38-2 no. 9567 awaits its next assignment at Harahan, La., in February 1990.

The only modifications I made to the underbody were to file off the casting marks on the fuel tank and to install a speed recorder on the lead axle on the left-hand side.

PAINTING

I found that painting was the easiest part of this project. First I washed the shell in mild dishwashing detergent to remove any oil that might be left on it from handling. Since Scalecoat II is plastic-compatible, no primer was necessary. I used Scalecoat II Loco Black, but you may wish to add a small amount of white paint to increase the visibility of details. Then, after mixing the paint 50:50 with Scalecoat II Thinner, I sprayed the body shell, fuel tank, detached truck sideframes, and handrail assemblies.

After the black had dried thoroughly, I added a coat of Pactra Crystal Clear to provide a high-gloss finish for decals. This isn't entirely necessary, since Scalecoat II dries to a gloss finish, but I wanted to make sure that the surface was completely smooth before adding decals. I gave the fuel tank, truck sideframes, and handrails a coat of Testor's Dullcote. Next, I brush-painted the outer face of the wheels flat black before reattaching the truck sideframes.

I followed Microscale's directions to apply the decals using Micro Set and Micro Sol. The only tricky part of this step is applying the white stripe to the ends of the unit. The top area of the pilot bulges out in the center, making it difficult to place the stripe across it. I positioned a short piece of the stripe on each side of the bulge and then cut the

Fig. 1 DETAILS

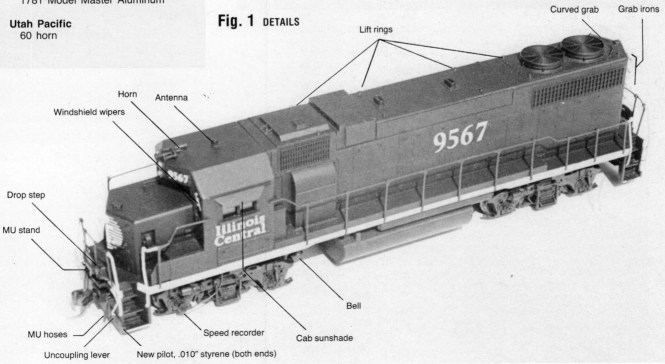

Curved grab · Grab irons · Lift rings · Horn · Antenna · Windshield wipers · Drop step · MU stand · MU hoses · Uncoupling lever · New pilot, .010" styrene (both ends) · Speed recorder · Cab sunshade · Bell

F.M. Patty, Jr.

This head-on photograph shows IC's corporate logo and two different number board styles.

inside edge to match. This was followed by a thin stripe underneath the protrusion. One alternative to this would be to just paint this area by hand.

Finishing the Model

After the decals were fully set and dry, I rinsed the decal areas with water and quickly dried them to remove any water spots or decal glue residue. Now it was time to install the grab irons on the nose and brush-paint them black, add the handrails, and do any necessary touch-up painting. Then I gave the whole body a coat of Dullcote.

I painted the ends of the handrails and uncoupling levers white, using Testor's Model Master Flat White because it covers well. Next, I painted the m.u. hose glad hands with Model Master Aluminum. You can now add the couplers to the body and attach the body (without the windshield piece) to the frame.

I weathered the engine by spraying it with a light coat of Scalecoat II Loco Grime, although in the few months after the prototype's trip to the paint shop it had acquired much more weathering. A coat of Dullcote sealed everything.

Finally, I detached the body, installed the windshield, and reattached the body to the frame. The windshield wipers and headlight lenses could be added. I prefer silver windshield wipers rather than the prototype's black because they show up better. My unit was ready to be put to work.

Union Pacific GP20

A leading "second generation" diesel in HO scale

SECOND GENERATION is a term used broadly to describe a lot of diesel locomotives, but there's a good argument for calling the GP20 the first second-generation diesel. Electro-Motive promoted it as a replacement for the diesels built during and immediately after World War II, locomotives which were due for major overhauls when the GP20 was introduced.

In the middle 1950s the Union Pacific wanted more horsepower in a four-axle road switcher. One way to increase power was to add a turbocharger to the 1,750-hp diesel of the GP9, boosting its output to 2,000-hp. The UP began to experiment with turbocharged GP9s in 1955, and upgraded a number of its 300-series GP9s this way in the years between 1959 and 1966.

Meanwhile, Electro-Motive began its own turbocharger program in 1956, and cooperated with the UP's efforts. Then in 1959, EMD introduced the 2,000-hp GP20. The GP20 shared the basic layout and overall dimensions of the GP7, GP9, and GP18. The most distinctive external features of the GP20 are the rectangular bulges on each side behind the cab, which house the air intakes for the turbocharger. Also, it has a single large exhaust stack directly above the turbocharger, instead of the two small stacks above the engine of the "normally aspirated" (nonturbo) Geeps.

The Union Pacific purchased 30 GP20s in 1960, nos. 700-729. They came with all the usual Union Pacific options including dynamic brakes, m.u. equipment, and a winterization hatch over the 36" radiator fan.

Numbers 700-729 were renumbered as 470-499 in December of 1962, but they remained the only true GP20s on the UP roster. The railroad's GP9 upgrading program was providing similar units, and in 1961 EMD introduced the 2,250-hp GP30. But the GP20s were successful locomotives and served the Union Pacific into the early 1980s.

Besides the UP, GP20 purchasers included the Atchison, Topeka & Santa Fe; Chicago, Burlington & Quincy; Great Northern (high nose); New York Central; Southern Pacific and its subsidiary St. Louis-Southwestern; and Western Pacific (high nose). Through mergers, GP20s also found their way onto the rosters of the Burlington Northern and the Penn Central.

Paul Schneider photo: Doug Nuckles collection

Union Pacific GP20 no. 496 was little changed from her original condition when photographed at Green River, Wyo., in March of 1977. The turbocharged B-B was built in 1960.

An HO Model

I'll describe an easy-to-make GP20 with UP characteristics. For this project, the undecorated plastic body shell from Proto Power West is ideal. If you have to start with a painted Mantua (or Tyco) body, soak it in brake fluid for a few hours, then scrub with a toothbrush to remove the loosened paint. When the shell is thoroughly clean, rinse it well in warm water with just a little dishwashing detergent.

Cut off the two plastic mounting posts projecting under the body and trim away the inside ribs to let the body fit down onto the mechanism. An Athearn motor or the Proto Power West can motor will easily fit inside the body.

The Mantua trucks were held in place in the four slots in the body. Fill the slots with .060" styrene and sand the filled areas smooth.

To attach the shell to the chassis, I drilled a .030"-diameter hole through the side sill above the air reservoir on each side and into the metal underframe. Then I cemented .030" steel pins into the underframe with CA (cyanoacrylate adhesive). The pins stick out just far enough to fit into the sills and hold the body in place. I also drilled No. 50 holes through the coupler mounts on the underframes and tapped them for 2-56 machine screws to secure the Kadee no. 5 couplers in their own insulating boxes.

The detailing for a UP GP20 is shown in fig. 1. The exhaust stack should be in line with the rear of the intake bulges on the sides of the hood, so it's best to remove the original stack and replace it.

I used dynamic brake parts from a scrap Athearn GP9 shell, but you could use the Mantua part with the Proto Power shell. The brake fan could be replaced with a Details West no. 144 pantop fan for greater accuracy, and you might also want to use the Details West no. 145 flared-shroud 48" radiator fans.

Union Pacific Paint

The UP GP20s were painted in the long-standard Armour Yellow and Harbor Mist Gray paint scheme as shown in fig. 2. Yellow paint doesn't cover black plastic very well, but with this scheme the Harbor Mist Gray can be the primer.

First install the Mantua handrails, securing the stanchions to the railings with a small drop of CA at each joint, but don't cement the railings or stanchions to the body. Then airbrush everything with Floquil Harbor Mist Gray and allow this paint to dry.

Bill of materials

Athearn
4200 GP35 chassis*

Detail Associates
1301 sunshades
1401 drop steps
1502 m.u. stands
1508 m.u. hoses
1703 clear jewels
1802 whip antenna
2202 grab irons
2205 uncoupling levers
2206 eyebolts
2403 turbo exhaust stack

Details West
126 beacon
164 winterization hatch
173 horn

Evergreen styrene
9010 .010" sheet
9040 .040" sheet
9060 .060" sheet

Floquil paints
110004 Crystal-Cote
110040 Dark Green
110100 Old Silver
110166 Armour Yellow
110167 Harbor Mist Gray

Kadee
No. 5 couplers

Mantua
2257 GP20 body shell*
10068 GP20 handrail set

Microscale decals
87-35 UP freight diesels no. 1 (We can handle it)*
87-36 UP freight diesels no. 2 (DEPENDABLE TRANSPORTATION)*
87-110-5 3" and 4¾" red stripes

Precision Scale Co.
3968 windshield wipers

Proto Power West
55519 GP20 chassis*
55521 undecorated Mantua GP20 body with dynamic brake parts*

Testors
1160 Dullcote

Trackside Parts
42 air reservoirs

* Indicates options or alternative sources

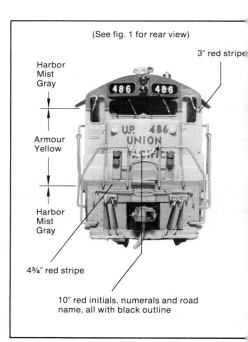

Rear end like front except as noted

Clear jewels used for headlight and class lights

Grab irons, 6

486 486

U.P. 486

Pilot left open to allow removal of body

(See fig. 1 for rear view)

3" red stripe

Harbor Mist Gray

486 486

U.P. 486
UNION PACIFIC

Armour Yellow

Harbor Mist Gray

4¾" red stripe

10" red initials, numerals and road name, all with black outline

Next remove the painted handrail-and-stanchion assemblies and mask off the body areas that are to remain gray. Spray the top of the nose with Floquil Dark Green, to represent the UP's non-skid green antiglare panel, and mask this panel too when dry. Now spray the rest of the body with Floquil Armour Yellow, let this dry to the touch, and remove all masking. Spray the body with an overall coat of Floquil Crystal-Cote for a protective layer, which is also a good surface for the decals. While waiting for this to dry, airbrush the truck sideframes with Floquil Old Silver.

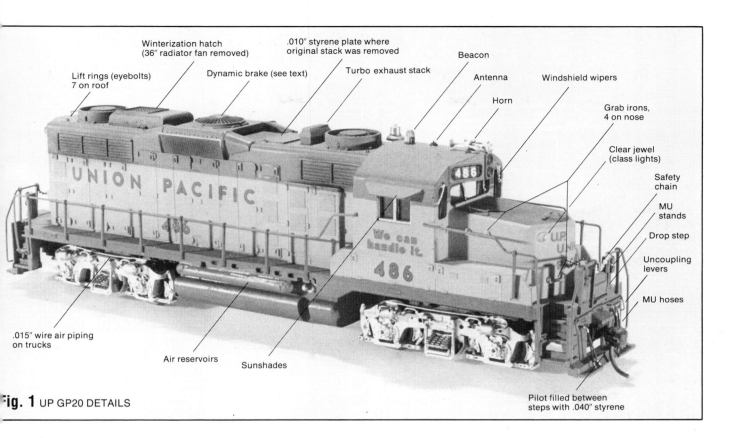

Lift rings (eyebolts)
7 on roof

Winterization hatch
(36" radiator fan removed)

.010" styrene plate where
original stack was removed

Dynamic brake (see text)

Turbo exhaust stack

Beacon

Antenna

Horn

Windshield wipers

Grab irons,
4 on nose

Clear jewel
(class lights)

Safety
chain

MU
stands

Drop step

Uncoupling
levers

MU hoses

.015" wire air piping
on trucks

Air reservoirs

Sunshades

Pilot filled between
steps with .040" styrene

Fig. 1 UP GP20 DETAILS

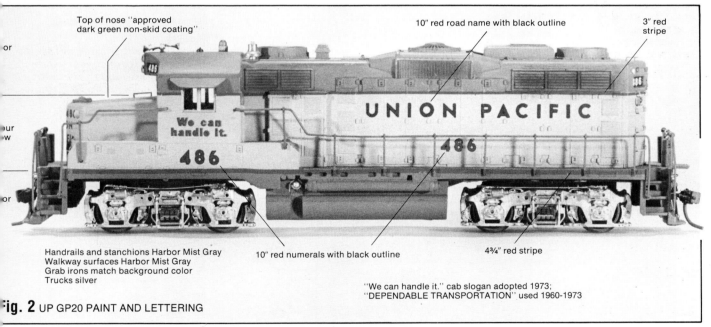

Top of nose "approved
dark green non-skid coating"

10" red road name with black outline

3" red
stripe

Handrails and stanchions Harbor Mist Gray
Walkway surfaces Harbor Mist Gray
Grab irons match background color
Trucks silver

10" red numerals with black outline

4¾" red stripe

"We can handle it." cab slogan adopted 1973;
"DEPENDABLE TRANSPORTATION" used 1960-1973

Fig. 2 UP GP20 PAINT AND LETTERING

Lettering and Finish

Microscale set no. 87-35 provides all the lettering you'll need for this model; set 87-36 has the earlier cab slogan, "DEPENDABLE TRANSPORTATION." The striping comes from set 87-110-5.

When all the decals are set, reinstall the handrails and do any touchup required with a small red sable brush. Then spray the body with Testor's Dullcote to seal the decals and give it a smooth, flat finish.

I applied a little light weathering with a mixture of black and gray powdered chalk, mostly around the fans and grills, for a slightly used appearance. The headlight lenses, class light jewels, and cabwindow glazing were also added. Assemble the body chassis, and sideframes, and this Geep is ready to work the railroad.
— *Doug Nuckles*

Wisconsin Central SD45

Modeling the WC's maroon and yellow scheme

BY LANCE BURTON

PHOTOS BY A. L. SCHMIDT

*I*N OCTOBER 1987, *Wisconsin Central Ltd. began operations with a fleet of SD45s purchased from the Burlington Northern, Southern Pacific, and Norfolk & Western. Several were subsequently rebuilt and repainted at the road's North Fond du Lac, Wis., shops.*

THE WISCONSIN CENTRAL has tried three versions of its maroon and yellow paint scheme. The "Christmas Tree" scheme, which was introduced in the summer of 1988, is currently the official color scheme.

Some of the first SD45s repainted in Wisconsin Central colors were former Norfolk & Western high-hood units in the 1700 series. These aren't actually owned by the WC but by the Oxford Group, a leasing organization. Since

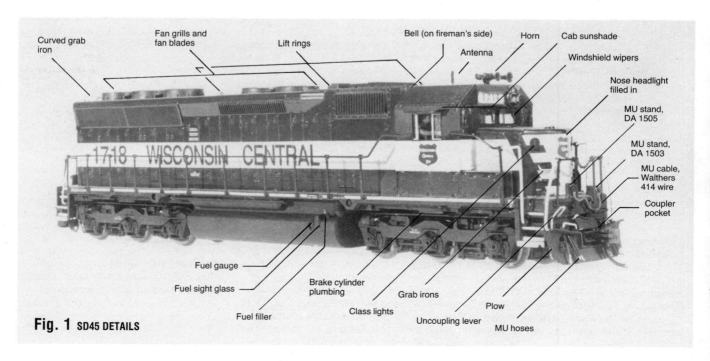

Fig. 1 SD45 DETAILS

Curved grab iron — Fan grills and fan blades — Lift rings — Bell (on fireman's side) — Horn — Cab sunshade — Antenna — Windshield wipers — Nose headlight filled in — MU stand, DA 1505 — MU stand, DA 1503 — MU cable, Walthers 414 wire — Coupler pocket — Fuel gauge — Fuel sight glass — Brake cylinder plumbing — Grab irons — Fuel filler — Class lights — Uncoupling lever — Plow — MU hoses

Chinese Red and gray U25B

Modeling one of the CB&Q's first non-EMD road diesels

GENERAL ELECTRIC scored a major coup in 1964 when the Chicago, Burlington & Quincy added six GE U25Bs, nos. 100-105, to its roster. The units, delivered in October 1964, were the Burlington's first non-EMD road diesels. They were painted in the road's distinctive Chinese Red and light gray paint scheme, which had been standard since 1959.

As a modeler of the late-1960s Burlington, I figured a U25B or two would be a nice addition to my motive-power roster. The Stewart Hobbies HO scale U25B is a nice model, with its see-through radiator screens, so it seemed a natural choice as a starting point. The Stewart model of the early U25B, with the large front windshield, is a close match to the Q's units. However, a few changes had to be made and details added before it was ready to be painted.

COUPLERS, HANDRAILS, AND OTHER DETAILS

I began by disassembling the cab, deck, and body. I used putty to fill the old air-horn hole in the roof, then located and drilled mounting holes for the grab irons, windshield wipers, m.u. hoses, and antenna. Figure 1 shows how I added the nose headlight. I used a sharp hobby knife and needle files to open a hole for the styrene block. Once it fit snugly, I fixed it in place with liquid plastic cement. I used the Stewart lenses for the upper headlights, but to hold the new headlight I added a 1/2"-long piece of 3/16"-square brass tubing to the inside roof of the cab directly behind the lenses.

I chose to mount the couplers on the body instead of the frame, filling the opening on the pilot as shown in fig. 2. I used a hacksaw to remove the coupler extension from each end of the frame. I drilled a no. 52 clearance hole in the new coupler mounting pads to clear the mounting screws and assembled and test-fit the Kadee coupler pockets. Satisfied with the fit, I used 400-grit sandpaper to smooth the joints between the pad, filler, and body.

The front and rear handrails supplied by Stewart are the two-part type. On prototype locomotives, these were connected with a chain, allowing crew members to pass between units. The Burlington's units were delivered with that type of handrail, but soon were replaced by solid ones. Making them was fairly simple. I used .019" brass rod, bending it according to a template. You can use the one shown in fig. 2. After bending the handrail, I polished the pieces at the joints with a Bright Boy. Then I used masking tape to secure the pieces in place on a block of wood. I soldered the stanchions in place and cleaned up the joints with a needle file.

I removed the truck sideframes from the model and added a speed recorder on the right side of the unit on the lead axle. The fuel fillers and air horn were made as shown in fig. 2. Shortly after completing the model, I discovered that

This Burlington U25B was two years old in this July 1966 scene at North Kansas City, Mo.

Custom Finishing makes a shrouded horn of this type. You'll find it listed in the bill of materials.

Next, I installed the grab irons, securing them with cyanoacrylate adhesive (CA). Once all the bodywork was done, I washed the body and let it air-dry.

PAINTING

I used Floquil paints, mixing them according to their formula of 75 percent paint, 20 percent Dio-Sol, and 5 percent Glaze. I began by spraying the shell, deck, and cab with a 15:1 mix of D&H Gray and Engine Black. I also used this mix to paint the hood ladder, horn, roof screen bracket, and cab sunshades.

After allowing this to dry for a few days, I masked the roof on the hood and cab. I used strips of masking tape, placed on a sheet of glass and cut lengthwise with a sharp knife. The cut edges help ensure a clean mask line. I applied the mask so the gray extended a scale 2'-3" down from the top of the tall doors on the hood. I also masked the hood ladder at the same height.

I used a mix of 3 parts Signal Red and 2 parts Railbox Yellow to spray the body, handrails, side screen brackets, and brake wheel.

Once the paint on the deck had dried, I masked it for the white stripe and sprayed it with Reefer White. I used a brush to paint the dynamic brake grids Grimy Black. After this had dried, I sprayed the body with Crystal-Cote to give a good surface for applying decals.

While waiting for the paint to dry on the body, I sprayed the truck sideframes, air tanks, bell, m.u. hoses, uncoupling levers, fuel fillers, and screens with a 1:1 mix of Engine Black and Grimy Black. I brush-painted the sides of the wheels with Grimy Black and the exposed metal areas behind the truck sideframes with Engine Black. I also brush-painted the remaining details: silver and black for the windshield wipers and antenna and a dab of silver to the fuel filler caps. I used a fine brush to paint the number boards Engine Black.

When the red paint on the handrails had dried, I brush-painted the corner posts with Engine Black. This might look rather strange, but the Q's GEs all featured red handrails with black corner posts. This was a variation from their EMD hood units, which had all-black handrails.

I installed the GRS Micro-Liting constant brightness unit according to their

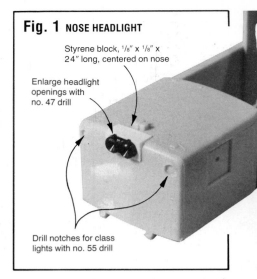

Fig. 1 NOSE HEADLIGHT

Styrene block, ¹⁄₈" x ¹⁄₈" x 24" long, centered on nose

Enlarge headlight openings with no. 47 drill

Drill notches for class lights with no. 55 drill

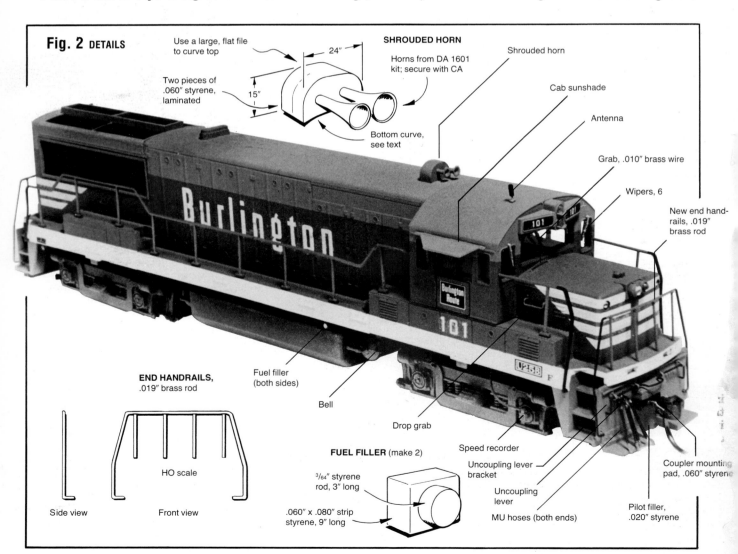

Fig. 2 DETAILS

Use a large, flat file to curve top

24"

15"

Two pieces of .060" styrene, laminated

Bottom curve, see text

SHROUDED HORN

Horns from DA 1601 kit; secure with CA

Shrouded horn

Cab sunshade

Antenna

Grab, .010" brass wire

Wipers, 6

New end handrails, .019" brass rod

END HANDRAILS, .019" brass rod

Fuel filler (both sides)

Bell

Drop grab

Speed recorder

Uncoupling lever bracket

Uncoupling lever

MU hoses (both ends)

Pilot filler, .020" styrene

Coupler mounting pad, .060" styrene

HO scale

Side view   Front view

FUEL FILLER (make 2)

³⁄₆₄" styrene rod, 3" long

.060" x .080" strip styrene, 9" long

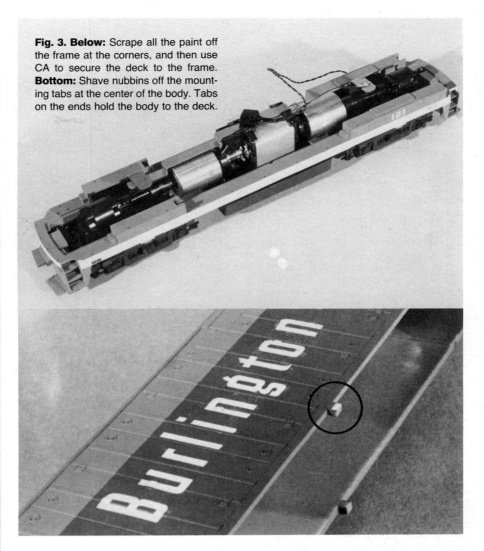

Fig. 3. Below: Scrape all the paint off the frame at the corners, and then use CA to secure the deck to the frame. **Bottom:** Shave nubbins off the mounting tabs at the center of the body. Tabs on the ends hold the body to the deck.

structions. When the shell is added to the frame, the bulb can be threaded into place in the brass tubing. It will stay in place without glue.

DECALS

I kept the hood, cab, and body separate when applying decals. The Microscale decals are quite thin, so I was careful to leave them on the backing paper after soaking them. I began with the large "Burlington" on the side, using a soft brush to add water to the decal and slide it into position. Then I blotted it with a paper towel and applied some Walthers Solvaset to get it to snuggle into the details. After it had dried, I used a sharp hobby knife to poke any air bubbles, then reapplied Solvaset to those areas.

Applying the nose and rear-end stripes was tricky. Because the hood slopes in at the corners, the stripes must be cut at the corner and applied in two pieces to keep them parallel with the deck. I also cut the decals where the stripes cross the indentation for the brake wheel on the left side of the nose. Note that the rear of the hood has only three stripes.

The Microscale decals were a little too tall to fit in the front number boards. For these I substituted numbers from Microscale set no. 87-90 for Burlington F units. The GE builder's plate is from set no. 87-48. After applying the decals, I gave the body a coat of Testor's Dullcote.

FINAL DETAILS

I used pieces of .010" clear styrene to add "glass" to the cab windows, making sure the styrene didn't interfere with the fit of the hood. I test-fit the hood, cab, and deck assembly, and when satisfied with the fit I removed the hood and cab from the deck and cemented the cab to the hood.

The body was originally attached to the frame by screws inserted through the coupler pockets. Since these were removed from the frame, I glued the deck to the frame with CA as shown in fig. 3. I also removed the nubbins on the side-mounting tabs of the hood. This lets the tabs on the ends of the body hold it in place on the frame, and allows removal of the body for maintenance.

After the body was in place, I added the remaining details. I used CA to mount the bell on the underframe and to mount the headlight and class light lenses. Note that the left nose headlight is red and the right one is clear.

I weathered the unit slightly, spraying the trucks and underframe with Dust, mixed 1:1 with Dio-Sol. I sprayed a thin (5 parts thinner, 1 part paint) Grimy Black mix around the exhaust stack and radiator screen areas. Now my unit was ready to be placed on the point of the next fast freight out of Lincoln. ◊

Central RR of New Jersey RS-3 in HO scale

Modeling a green and yellow locomotive of the 1950s

BY CHUCK DAVIS
PHOTOS BY THE AUTHOR

THE CENTRAL RR of New Jersey's dark green and yellow scheme was ushered in by a delivery of Alco RS-3 diesels in 1950. This scheme lasted on CNJ diesels well into the 1960s. Here's Chuck Davis to explain how he modeled one of these early diesels.

I GREW UP in Pennsylvania's Wyoming Valley during the 1950s and '60s, near the CNJ's large yard and car shops at Ashley. During this time the Central's green road and cab units, with their distinctive twin yellow stripes, were a common sight. Among these were pairs of Alco RS-3s assigned as pushers for the long climb from Ashley to Penobscot Yard at the top of the mountain and for mine runs on the

Nanticoke Branch. Single RS-3s handled many of the yard chores, mine runs, and locals.

This paint scheme replaced the blue and tangerine combination applied a year earlier to the Fairbanks-Morse H-15-44s. The green and yellow scheme lasted until 1962, when the stripes were deleted as part of a cost-cutting measure. However, units with stripes could be seen as late as 1968.

Central RR of New Jersey RS-3s were numbered 1540-1555 and 1700-1709. In 1945 the CNJ subleased all its Pennsylvania operations to the Central Railroad Co. of Pennsylvania, which was created to avoid New Jersey's high taxes. All locomotives and rolling stock assigned to the Pennsylvania Division, including RS-3s 1540-1544 and 1705-1709, carried "CRP" reporting marks until December 1, 1952, when the procedure was nullified by court action.

A fine series of articles by Richard Jahn in the Anthracite Railroads Historical Society publication *Flags, Diamonds and Statues* (1981-82) provides extensive background information on CNJ diesel paint schemes with their many minor variations. The book *Jersey Central Diesels* (Withers Publishing)

John M. Petko

CNJ Phase IIb RS-3 no. 1554, restored by the Hawk Mountain Chapter of the National Railway Historical Society, pulls a passenger excursion train at Jim Thorpe, Pa., in July of 1985.

also provides photos, rosters, paint diagrams, and a unit-by-unit chart of the various paint schemes.

Fortunately for HO modelers, Raritan Bay Hobbies (P. O. Box 4231, Metuchen, NJ 08840-4231; 908-494-2932) has designed and produced a series of decals to accurately model any of these units. They also offer custom-mixed Scalecoat II model paints, including the CNJ's unique shade of green. It was developed from an original 1950s-era sample taken from the Elizabethport, N. J., shops.

MODELING

I decided to use Stewart Hobbies' initial HO scale RS-3 version, an undecorated Phase Ib with punched louvers in the side doors, to model unit 1545. Stewart's newer Phase IIa kit, with horizontal box filters in the side doors, is a closer match to the CNJ's later RS-3 deliveries (nos. 1548 and up).

The major alteration was to the tank area of the frame, as shown in fig. 1. I replaced the kit's end railings with Smokey Valley Railroad & Machine Co. railings, but used the kit's handrail stanchions. I removed these from the handrail assembly and drilled them to accept new railings made from .015″ brass wire.

Before attaching the cab to the body, I traced the window openings on .030″ clear styrene, cut out and filed the clear windows until they fit tightly, and set them aside. The model's cab has two windows on one side and three on the other. On CNJ units, the three windows were offset or replaced by two centered windows. I didn't realize this until I finished the project, so I didn't try to correct it.

The most distinctive details of the CNJ RS-3s were their pedestal marker lights. A reasonable assembly can be made as shown in fig. 2. Using an oval needle file and 400-grit sandpaper, carefully file the base to fit snugly against the curved top of the hood. Attach the marker to the base with cyanoacrylate adhesive (CA) so that one lens opening is flush against the 1 x 8 back. Use liquid plastic cement to glue the assembly to the hood.

I formed the nose grab irons from .012″ brass wire, and added other details as shown in fig. 3.

I considerably improved the model's appearance and performance by replacing the wheels with NorthWest Short Line nickel-plated wheels.

In my opinion, the most significant improvement in the performance of the Stewart mechanism came from spraying good ol' WD-40 into the gearboxes and on the drive-shaft bearings. I recently learned this simple yet very effective procedure from a longtime acquaintance, R. L. Warren.

After finishing this work, I washed the shell with a mild soap and let it dry.

Fig. 1. AIR AND FUEL TANKS. The new air tanks are ¼″ Plastruct tubing, with .020″ styrene ends. The tank straps are 1 x 3 styrene strip, and the new fuel-tank faces are .020″ styrene.

PAINTING

I sprayed the shell (interior and exterior), frame, and trucks with Floquil Primer. Then I sprayed the trucks and frame with a 1:1 mix of Engine Black and Weathered Black (thinned for spraying).

I followed Raritan Bay's excellent directions and thinned their CNJ Green 25 percent with Scalecoat II thinner. After masking the cab interior, I sprayed the entire shell. This was the first time I had used Scalecoat II, and I was really impressed with the results. It's safe for plastics, gives excellent coverage, dries quicker than regular Scalecoat paint, and has a high-gloss surface ready for decal application.

I painted several of the smaller parts and set them aside to dry. This included spraying the couplers with Floquil Rust, and brush-painting the outer surface of the NWSL wheels and the wiper blades with Weathered Black and the handrails with Pactra Flat Insignia Yellow.

DECALS

Raritan Bay's CNJ-4 decal set provides enough heralds, numbers, and lettering to finish any two units, but only enough of the paired 7″ stripes with correct 11″ spacing to finish one. I began by applying the easier pieces first. The 30″ herald, numbers, and "CRP" letters on the cab (I didn't yet have the list of prototype CRP units when I lettered my model) were followed by the 18″ herald and smaller numbers on each end. Then I applied the "FPSD-46" class designation, fuel, and water fill lettering to the side sill.

The tedious task of applying the stripes is made much easier by starting with the straight sections. I attached a scale 7-foot-long section of double stripes to each side of the short hood and a 25-foot-long section on each side of the long hood. The lower stripe is positioned 46″ above the walkway. With the exception of a short segment of the paired stripes for use to check spacing, I cut the

remaining decals into individual stripes. I used an X-acto no. 11 blade and a metal straightedge to ensure that the cut edges of the decals wouldn't tear. I sharpened the blade on 600-grit sandpaper after every few cuts.

I cut two pieces 7 feet long for each side to start the striping through the radiator area. I used several applications of Solvaset and opened any air pockets with the no. 11 blade to get the decals into all the crevices in this area. It also

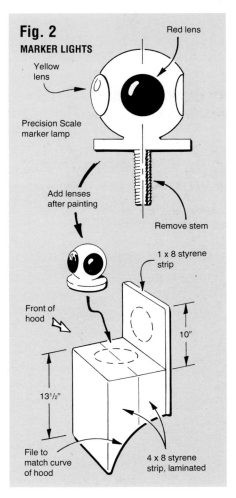

Fig. 2
MARKER LIGHTS

Red lens

Yellow lens

Precision Scale marker lamp

Add lenses after painting

Remove stem

Front of hood

1 x 8 styrene strip

10″

13½″

File to match curve of hood

4 x 8 styrene strip, laminated

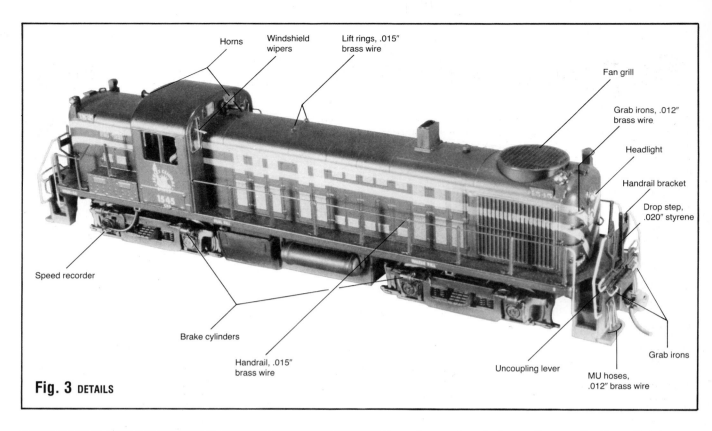

Horns
Windshield wipers
Lift rings, .015" brass wire
Fan grill
Grab irons, .012" brass wire
Headlight
Handrail bracket
Drop step, .020" styrene
Speed recorder
Brake cylinders
Handrail, .015" brass wire
Uncoupling lever
MU hoses, .012" brass wire
Grab irons

Fig. 3 DETAILS

Bill of materials

Champion decal
S-67 6" HO black stripes

Detail Associates
1012 headlight
2205 uncoupling lever
2504 .012" brass wire
2505 .015" brass wire
2703 cooling fan grill
2801 brake cylinders

Details West
166 fuel filler
173 horn

Evergreen Scale Models styrene
8103 1 x 3 HO scale strip
8108 1 x 8 HO scale strip
8408 4 x 8 HO scale strip
9020 .020" plain sheet

Floquil paint
110009 Primer
110010 Engine Black
110017 Weathered Black
110073 Rust
110086 Grime

Kadee
5 couplers

K&S Engineering
306 .030" clear plastic sheet

Labelle Industries
7001 figures

MV Products
19 clear and red lenses
220 red lenses
222 amber lenses

NorthWest Short Line
7140-4 replacement wheels

Pactra Acrylic Enamel paint
1127 Insignia Yellow

Plastruct
608 1/4" round tubing

Precision Scale Co.
31634 round marker lamps, 2

Raritan Bay Hobbies
CNJ-5 CNJ road switcher decals
CNJ-200 CNJ Green paint

Scalecoat paint
51 Flat Glaze

Smokey Valley
P109 end handrails

Stewart
1000 RS-3, Phase Ib

Utah Pacific
61 speed recorder
94 windshield wipers

Walthers
470 Solvaset
2540 White Railroad Roman decals

took another application of stripes to cover some of the irregular surfaces.

Next I opted to finish the lower stripe on each end by trial and error. Without applying Solvaset, two pieces 36" long were angled sharply on each end to form the "V." I formed the curved sections by making cuts halfway through a long piece about every scale 3", creating a fan effect. I first cut a single piece long enough to complete the right side. When satisfied with the fit, I applied Solvaset to the "V" first, then the curved section. The curved section on the left must be pieced to fit around the grab irons. I completed the upper stripe using the short section of paired stripes to check the spacing.

I made the number boards by applying pieces of 6" black stripe 21" long. After the Solvaset had dried, I added numbers cut from a Walthers Railroad Roman number set. Raritan Bay set CNJ-5 can also be used — it has the correct number series to minimize decal splicing.

When I was satisfied that all the air bubbles had been removed, I sprayed the shell with Scalecoat Flat Glaze. Since I model the period shortly after the RS-3s were introduced in 1950, I weathered this unit lightly. I sprayed thinned Weathered Black around the stack and top of the hood, and thinned Grime on the trucks and steps.

After completing the painting, I installed the window material and MV lenses using diluted white glue. With the addition of the crew, engine no. 1545 brings back fond memories of a powerful workhorse. ۵

Suppliers and Manufacturers

When writing for information, be sure to include a self-addressed, stamped enelope. Some firms offer free catalogs or literature; others charge for their catalogs. Some railroads suppliers will sell direct to consumers; others sell only through hobby shops. Always check with your local hobby shop before attempting to order direct from a manufacturer or importer. If you don't have a hobby shop in your area, there a number of firms that sell parts and equipment by mail order.

A-Line (Proto Power West)
1760 White Ave.
La Verne, CA 91750
HO scale diesel locomotive components, detail parts, and decals.

Accu-paint (SMP Industries)
63 Hudson Rd., P. O. Box 72
Bolton, MA 01740
HO scale decals and paints.

Athearn
19010 Laurel Park Rd.
Compton, CA 90220
HO scale ready-to run locomotives.

Atlas Model Railroad Co.
378 Florence Ave.
Hillside, NJ 07205
N and HO scale locomotives.

Builders In Scale
P. O. Box 441432
Aurora, CO 80044
HO scale kits and accessories.

Cannon & Co.
310 Willow Heights
Aptos, CA 95003-9798
HO scale diesel component kits.

Con-Cor International
8101 E. Research Ct.
Tucson, AZ 85710
N and HO scale locomotives.

Detail Associates
P. O. Box 5357
San Luis Obispo, CA 93403
Detail parts in HO, O, and N.

Details West
P. O. Box 5132
Hacienda Heights, CA 91745
HO scale detail parts.

Evergreen Scale Models, Inc.
12808 Northeast 125th Way
Kirkland, WA 98034
Styrene building materials.

Floquil-Polly S Color Corp.
4615 St. Hwy 30 N
Amsterdam, NY 12010-9204
Color coatings for railroading.

Grandt Line Products Inc.
1040-B Shary Ct.
Concord, CA 94518
HO scale detail parts.

GRS Micro-Liting
P. O. Box 16063
Shawnee, KS 66203
Electronic components for all hobbies.

K&S Engineering
6917 West 59th St.
Chicago, IL 60638
Brass building materials.

Kadee Quality Products Co.
673 Ave. C
White City, OR 97503
Couplers, tools, and accessories.

Keystone Locomotive Works
P. O. Box J
Pulteney, NY 14874
HO scale locomotive kits.

Mantua Industries, Inc.
P. O. Box 10, Grandview Ave.
Woodbury Heights, NJ 08097
HO scale locomotives.

Microscale® Industries, Inc.
1570 Sunland Lane
Costa Mesa, CA 92626
Decals for all hobbies.

Miniatronics Corp.
561-K Acorn St.
Deer Park, NY 11729
Electronic components.

Model Power
180 Smith St.
Farmingdale, NY 11735
HO scale locomotive kits.

NorthWest Short Line
Box 423
Seattle, WA 98111
Mechanisms and components for model railroading.

Overland Models Inc.
5908 Kilgore Ave.
Muncie, IN 47304
Imported scale locomotives and parts.

Pactra Inc.
620 Buckbee St.
Rockford, IL 61104
Hobby paints.

Plastruct Inc.
1020 South Wallace Pl.
City of Industry, CA 91748
Plastic building materials.

Precision Scale Co., Inc.
3961 Highway 93 N., Box 288
Stevensville, MT 59870
Imported scale locomotives and parts.

Run 8 Productions
P. O. Box 25224
Rochester, NY 14625
HO scale windows for locomotives.

ShellScale Decals
2140 Houston Mines Rd.
Troutville, VA 24175
Decals for model railroading.

Smokey Valley Railroad Products
P. O. Box 339
Plantersville, MS 38862
HO scale locomotive kits and detail parts.

Stewart Hobbies Inc.
P. O. Box 341
Chalfont, PA 18914
HO scale locomotives.

Testor Corporation
620 Buckbee St.
Rockford, IL 61104
Paints and finishing materials.

Utah Pacific (Tomar Industries)
9520 East Napier Ave.
Benton Harbor, MI 49022
HO scale brass diesel detail parts.

Virnex Industries
S-2083 Herwig Rd.
Reedsburg, WI 53959
N and HO scale metal and wood kits.

Woodland Scenics
P. O. Box 98
Linn Creek, MO 65052
Dry transfer graphics for model railroading.

William K. Walthers, Inc.
P. O. Box 18676
Milwaukee, WI 53218
Manufacturer and distributor of model railroad products in all scales. Publishes a catalog and reference manual, *The World of HO Scale.*

Index